Learning Online

TECH.edu

A Hopkins Series on Education and Technology

LEARNING ONLINE

The Student Experience

George Veletsianos

JOHNS HOPKINS UNIVERSITY PRESS | *Baltimore*

Johns Hopkins University Press
2715 North Charles Street
Baltimore, Maryland 21218-4363
www.press.jhu.edu

Cataloging-in-Publication Data is available from the Library of Congress.

A catalog record for this book is available from the British Library.

ISBN-13: 978-1-4214-3809-2 (hardcover)
ISBN-13: 978-1-4214-3810-8 (ebook)

Special discounts are available for bulk purchases of this book. For more information, please contact Special Sales at specialsales@press.jhu.edu.

Johns Hopkins University Press uses environmentally friendly book materials, including recycled text paper that is composed of at least 30 percent post-consumer waste, whenever possible.

To my family

CONTENTS

ACKNOWLEDGMENTS

This book owes its existence to learners: my students, learners I've interviewed, and learners who have shared their thoughts with other researchers, with the media, and with the world at large through their writing.

Throughout my career, I have been fortunate to interact with a network of peers and colleagues who have helped me make better sense of online learning. These individuals have helped me by writing on the topic, by critiquing early drafts of my work, by commenting on my work, by writing with me, and by interacting with me online and offline. They've also helped me by just being who they are, by doing creative, generous, and important scholarship. I am especially appreciative of the work of the following individuals in impacting my perspective: Joan Hughes, Kate Bowles, Audrey Watters, Laura Czerniewicz, Shandell Houlden, and Royce Kimmons. If you haven't had a chance to read their work, I highly recommend doing so.

This book would not have been possible without the support of my research assistants. Either by contributing directly to this work and/or indirectly supporting my research agenda; their help has been invaluable. Individuals contributing early research and writing directly to this work include Ash Shaw (who contributed to chapters 6, 14, 15, and 16) and Joelle Nagle (who contributed to chapters 2, 3, 4, 5, 7, 9, and 10).

Writing appearing in this book has appeared elsewhere in different formats, and, with permission, it is heavily edited and republished here. Specifically, the book draws from the following publications:

Chapter 11 draws from G. Veletsianos and R. Moe (2017), "The Rise of Educational Technology as a Sociocultural and Ideological Phenomenon," *Educause Review*, http://er.educause.edu/articles /2017/4/the-rise-of-educational-technology-as-a-sociocultural -and-ideological-phenomenon; and from G. Veletsianos and C. Miller (2008), "Conversing with Pedagogical Agents: A Phenomenological Exploration of Interacting with Digital Entities," *British Journal of Educational Technology* 39 (6): 969–986.

Chapter 12 draws from G. Veletsianos, A. Collier, and E. Schneider (2015), "Digging Deeper into Learners' Experiences in MOOCs: Participation in Social Networks Outside of MOOCs, Notetaking, and Contexts Surrounding Content Consumption," *British Journal of Educational Technology* 46 (3): 570–587.

Chapter 13 draws from G. Veletsianos (2012), "Higher Education Scholars' Participation and Practices on Twitter," *Journal of Computer Assisted Learning* 28 (4): 336–349; and from G. Veletsianos and C. Navarrete (2012), "Online Social Networks as Formal Learning Environments: Learner Experiences and Activities," *The International Review of Research in Open and Distance Learning* 13 (1): 144–166.

Introduction

In multiple conversations at multiple institutions over the years, I have heard educated, passionate, and good-willed people talk with excitement about the number of students participating in online and distance courses. More than a million students in Canada. More than 100,000 in the early massive open online courses (MOOCs), more than 20,000 in recent ones. More than 200 enrolled in a for-credit foundations course at a local university. Nearly two million online learners at one of the world's well-known open and mega university. While such figures are impressive, an enthusiastic and all-consuming focus on the numbers can lead us to lose sight of Irma, Magda, Hassan, James, and Asma; or of the reasons that Anna failed to complete her degree; or Nick and Cassandra who were compelled to enroll in higher education while raising a family. Nor is it just our fascination with scale and numbers that leads us astray. A variety of common discourses, practices, and pressures operate in similar ways to alienate us from students and their realities—such as the adoption of business-like language to refer to students as "prospects" or financial constraints that move us to prioritize goals like "competitiveness" and "growth" over more community-oriented or people-centered goals.

The future of higher education is at a crucial turning point. True, the university as an institution is facing immense pressures and a myriad of challenges, and various aspects of it are badly in need of tweaks, reform, and perhaps bottom-up rethinking. Online education, however, is not a panacea, but just one aspect of what higher education may look like in the future. To help create that future, I argue that the people involved in online education—instructors, researchers, administrators, instructional designers, directors of centers of teaching and learning, policymakers, entrepreneurs, technology developers, and higher education consultants—need to better understand the needs and experiences of our students. I include myself in this group, and for brevity's sake I will refer to this group as *we* throughout the book. We need to understand students as people, as individuals who have agency, desires, mishaps, dreams, life-changing accidents; as individuals who face the daily minutiae of life; and as people who may even have instructive and insightful ideas about the future of education. The purpose of this book, therefore, is to examine online learning through the lens of student experience and help us narrow our distance from the online students we serve.

To that end, the book is both descriptive and analytical. Each of the following chapters focuses on an important or noteworthy aspect of online learners' experiences by offering, first, an actual or composite story from an online student gathered from my own research and experiences or occasionally from other reports, followed by an analysis of that story that also examines and synthesizes some of the existing research on the theme. I was inspired to use this approach after reading *The Man Who Mistook His Wife for a Hat*, a book in which Dr. Oliver Sacks presented short narratives of patients with neurological disorders that enabled him to discuss various aspects of neurology. By offering a deeper understanding and appreciation of learner experiences—which Parrish (2005) describes as the ways learners interact with and respond to content, activities, instructional methods, instructors, and the context within which learning and instruction happen—this book is intended to help us learn more about our students and uncover ways we can refine and improve online teaching, learning, and education.

Online education has a distinctive quality, one that risks creating and widening the distance between us and our students. That quality is the physical distance that separates us from students and requires us to take active steps to build and foster our relationship with them. In online learning settings, students participate in courses from locations that are usually at a distance from the educational institution offering the course, typically through such activities as completing assignments at home, listening to an assigned podcast on a commute, or studying for an exam at a public library. This geographic dispersal is what advocates of online learning are referring to when they claim that online learning can take place "anywhere." In this context, courses may meet in real time (synchronous learning) or never meet in real time (asynchronous learning). Some online courses may meet on a regular and consistent basis much like conventional face-to-face courses, others may have optional scheduled meetings, and some may be asynchronous with optional one-on-one tutorials. In all these cases, learners' experiences take place at a distance from their instructors and classmates. This may even be true for online courses taken by students enrolled in predominantly face-to-face institutions, such as an online course offered to allow students from different majors to fulfill a requirement not offered by their own department.

By now, online learning has become ordinary and deeply embedded in the fabric of global society. In 2013, my primary care physician, for instance, praised Khan Academy and described to me how it had helped his son excel in math, a feat his classroom teachers had apparently failed to accomplish. A friend of mine recently completed a yearlong painting course taught online by an entrepreneurial artist. My students have included one who creates online training modules to help British Columbia employees monitor and report on the provincial election process and another who designs short-duration online courses for aspiring makeup artists. Recently, several of my Facebook friends were excited and were full of questions about a tennis class that Serena Williams was slated to teach via masterclass.com. Today students can enroll in online courses from a seemingly never-ending array of public, private, nonprofit, and for-profit educational institutions and credential providers. With online education being taken up in such extensive and diverse ways, it is imperative that educators better understand what it is like to be an online learner.

The current list of online education providers includes established and emerging institutions and companies that are vying for online learners, such as the University of Pennsylvania, the University of British Columbia, the University of Wisconsin–Madison, Western Governors' University, Southern New Hampshire University, Open Universities Australia, University of Phoenix, FutureLearn, University of the People, and Lynda.com, to name just a few. Little more than a decade ago, online learning was generally considered a poor cousin of face-to-face learning, as a format engaged in only by lower-tier universities or, worse yet, a vehicle for diploma mills. Yet online learning has come to play such a significant role in today's institutions of higher education that in a survey conducted in 2018, most Canadian post-secondary institutions reported having or developing an online learning strategy (72%) and considering online learning very or extremely important (68%) to their long-term strategic or academic plan (Canadian Digital Learning Association 2019). Recent surveys of US academic leaders show similar results, with about 63% reporting that they viewed online education as "critical to the long-term strategy" of their institution (Allen and Seaman 2016).

My own experiences with online education have also motivated me to write this book. I've had many positive experiences with online learning. I've taken online courses as a student, my favorite being a statistics course offered by the educational psychology department at the University of Minnesota. Over the past 11 years, I've taught a number of online courses at the University of Manchester (UK), the University of Texas at Austin (USA), and Royal Roads University (Canada). I've also extensively researched the topic and helped faculty and administrators (as well as my own students) launch and improve online learning offerings via courses, workshops, talks, keynotes, and one-to-one advice. But I'm also a serial dropout, having signed up for countless MOOCs but completing only a handful. In this, I'm not alone. Historically, online and distance learning courses have had high dropout rates (Peters 1992), and many online learners have reported feelings of isolation (Galusha 1997) and unsatisfying and impersonal interactions (Vonderwell 2003; Song et al. 2004; Paechter, Maier, and Macher 2010; Lee et al. 2011). My experiences as an online learner, online instructor, researcher of online learning, and consultant have afforded me a number of insights into online learning that I hope to relay in the pages that follow.

Although the expansion and ordinariness of online learning have made the field a growing area of interest among researchers who have amassed a large body of knowledge about online courses, the actual lived experiences of online learners have remained somewhat elusive. The current literature provides a paucity of in-depth, rich descriptions of the diverse day-to-day lived experiences of online learners. Although that literature contains many descriptions of learners' activities online, their beliefs about online learning, and their reasons for enrolling in or dropping out of online classes, little research has attempted to dig deep into the quotidian experiences of learners. The elusive nature of online learners' experiences is a problem because it prevents us from doing better: from designing more effective online courses, from making evidence-informed decisions about online education, and from coming to our work with the full sense of empathy that our students deserve.

Furthermore, most of what we do know about online learners and their experiences is scattered in specialist peer-reviewed journals and individual studies, which makes it difficult for most faculty, administrators, staff, designers, policymakers, and entrepreneurs to stay up to date and make sense of the landscape around online learning. Moreover, few empirical studies of online learning offer reports of students' experiences in their own words, and mass media stories about online learning tend to focus on extraordinary rather than representative cases. This book, in contrast, is an effort to provide researchers and practitioners with an accessible and in-depth synthesis of the diverse experiences of typical online learners. Its goal is to help us better understand what it is like to be an online student and thus to shorten the experiential distance between us and our students.

As suggested above, this effort is guided in large part by my hope that by listening to learners, by truly listening to what it is like and what it means and requires to be an online learner, we can improve teaching and learning. I conduct research to improve practice, and I am convinced that by adopting a pedagogical orientation in our research—one of empathy and compassion, of listening and caring—we can work with learners to foster empowering, equitable, effective, and truly inspiring learning experiences. I also believe that technology, when used in prosocial, critical, and ethical ways, can help us design experiences like these by removing barriers to access, connecting us with others, broadening our perspectives, and equipping us with a variety of tools to solve pressing educational problems.

But this book is also motivated by my irritation with several tendencies in current discourses surrounding digital education and online learning—particularly the suggestion that teaching and learning can be fully analyzed, understood, engineered, and redesigned simply by capturing, analyzing, and drawing inferences from the data that learners leave behind as they roam from one digital activity to the next. While analyses of the data trails of learners' participation on digital platforms may help us understand how students engage with online learning, such studies focus on users' activities and behaviors as opposed to their lived experiences and often reduce learners to numbers and statistics. Could such studies be helpful? Of course. But, the uncritical adoption of such methods may thus further distance us from, rather than bring us closer to, the actual experiences of our students. Despite such claims as "by collecting every click, homework submission, quiz, and forum note from tens of thousands of students, Coursera is a data mine that offers a new way to study learning" (May 2012) and that by tracing such data "we can see everything the students do" (Chu 2013), these vast amounts of data clearly represent only part of the activities that actually affect a student's learning. Students might, for instance, also print and read a paper offline, call classmates on the phone to discuss an assignment, or engage in a variety of actions that are invisible to digital learning platforms and tracking. Nor do such data capture all the psychological, social, and emotional factors that affect learning. Much of the current literature on online learning thus leaves me yearning to know more about the actual lives and experiences of online students. I fear that by making assumptions about such learners without understanding those experiences, we may be designing systems that do not necessarily reflect their needs or how their studies actually fit into their plans and lives. This is not a call for more data or different kinds of data, such as physiological data, but rather a call to use a wider variety of lenses to understand learners, online learning, and digital participation.

The result of these issues—the scattered literature, the focus on big data, the prevalence of algorithmic analysis of big data, and the belief that we can "see" all that students do—creates a chasm between the day-to-day realities of the students we teach and our professional and social aspirations for online education. My own practice and writing have been admittedly influenced by my deep belief that understanding learners better can help us design education better. As you read the following chapters, I hope that you will come to agree with me.

References

Allen, L., and Seaman, J. 2016. *Online Report Card: Tracking Online Education in the United States.* Wellesley, MA: Babson Survey Research Group.

Canadian Digital Learning Association. 2019. *Tracking Online and Distance Education in Canadian Universities and Colleges: 2018.* https://onlinelearningsurveycanada.ca/download/604/.

Chu, J. 2013. "Data from edX's First Course Offer Preliminary Insights into Online Learning." *MITNews.* http://newsoffice.mit.edu/2013/6002x-dataoffer-insights-into-online-learning-0611.

Galusha, J. M. 1997. "Barriers to Learning in Distance Education." *Interpersonal Computing and Technology* 5 (3–4): 6–14.

Lee, S. J., Srinivasan, S., Trail, T., Lewis, D., and Lopez, S. 2011. "Examining the Relationship among Student Perception of Support, Course Satisfaction, and Learning Outcomes in Online Learning." *Internet and Higher Education* 14 (3): 158–163.

May, K. T. 2012. "Completely Free Online Classes? Coursera.org Now Offering Courses from 16 Top Colleges." *TED Blog*, July 18. https://blog.ted.com/completely-free-online-classes-coursera-org-now-offering-courses-from-14-top-colleges/.

Paechter, M., Maier, B., and Macher, D. 2010. "Students' Expectations of, and Experiences in E-learning: Their Relation to Learning Achievements and Course Satisfaction." *Computers & Education* (1): 222–229.

Parrish, P. 2005. "Embracing the Aesthetics of Instructional Design." *Educational Technology* 45 (2): 16–25.

Peters, O. 1992. "Some Observations on Dropping Out in Distance Education." *Distance Education* 13 (2): 234–269.

Song, L., Singleton, E. S., Hill, J. R., and Koh, M. H. 2004. "Improving Online Learning: Student Perceptions of Useful and Challenging Characteristics." *Internet and Higher Education* 7 (1): 59–70.

Vonderwell, S. 2003. "An Examination of Asynchronous Communication Experiences and Perspectives of Students in an Online Course: A Case Study." *Internet and Higher Education* 6 (1): 77–90.

1.

The Learner Who Compared Online Courses to Face-to-Face Courses

Jim was a doctoral student at a large university located in the United States. In his day job, he served as the dean of teaching at a neighboring community college, responsible for evaluating and improving teaching practices. Jim's profile picture, in which he donned a red t-shirt and waved to the camera, aligned with the sense of warmth and hospitality that I got from his strong Southern accent. Because he had responded to a survey prior to our meeting, I had developed a mental picture of Jim's background: He was in his early fifties. He had access to a computer and mobile device at home and reported that he was comfortable using the internet to learn about topics of interest and to troubleshoot his devices. Even though he had a Facebook account, he almost never used it. He had also never used Twitter or uploaded a photo or video to a photo- or video-sharing website.

I was excited to talk with Jim because he had just completed his very first online course. Though my questions were about his experiences in the particular course he had taken, his responses seemed to naturally gravitate toward comparing those to his experiences in face-to-face courses. "I had a sharp learning curve," he admitted. "I'm new to online learning, so I didn't know what kind of expectations to have. I heard going into it that it's something that you have to stay on top of every moment or else you fall behind, which isn't always the case with traditional classes." The course he had just completed was compressed and therefore fast-paced, which required him to be online every day to complete daily activities that ranged from reading to writing reflections and responding to peers. He described it as "kind of like an intensive education," which he thought provided "greater depth into my studies, into my work in the course than I had in some of my traditional face-to-face courses." He reported engaging with his peers in a more active way than he was used to, which led him to the realization that physical copresence is not a necessary prerequisite for a high-quality learning experience. "It probably hit me toward the end of the first week. In a traditional face-to-face course, I don't always feel as connected to my classmates, even though I'm going to be sitting right next to them, engaged in face-to-face conversation. But [in the online course] by continually responding to their questions or asking questions of their assignments, I kind of felt a sense of connection. . . . It was a greater sense of connection than I thought I was going to have."

Listening to Jim describe his experiences reminded me of the many conversations and debates I have been involved in that ultimately boil down to whether face-to-face education is better than online education. I have had versions of this debate with colleagues, peer reviewers, students, and countless people I've met outside of work when they learned what I do in my research. I was also asked, during two separate job interviews, about why my research wasn't examining strategies that could ensure that online education is as good as face-to-face education. But as Jim had pinpointed with perfect clarity, the real issue is not whether online education is as "good" (whatever that means) as face-to-face education but instead how *this online course* differed in particular ways from *some* of the in-person courses he'd taken. We've all taken face-to-face courses that were more effective, engaging, inspiring, or harder or easier than others, which is true of online courses, too. And even though Jim reported spending his hour-long drive home from work wondering if "so-and-so responded to my discussion post" and did not "recall having that feeling in a face-to-face course," he most likely knew that some of his future online courses were going to be better than others in the same way that he had come to recognize that quality and modality weren't synonymous.

...

Can online education ever be as good as face-to-face education? This question has been debated ad nauseam. As I am writing this chapter, I am consulting with a university in the Caribbean, assisting faculty in converting some of their face-to-face courses to online ones, and I am anticipating that this question will arise during my workshops with faculty. The question is both predictable and understandable. Most faculty members have taught face-to-face courses and have a good understanding of the richness of an in-person classroom environment. Nevertheless, surveys of faculty members in the United States reveal that the majority have neither taught online nor taken an online course (Jaschik and Lederman 2018). The widely known and damning stories about predatory for-profit colleges and independent-study correspondence courses may, therefore, lead many of us to imagine that most contemporary online courses look like those. Gannon (2019, para. 5) writes that "so long as there are still predatory, for-profit, financial-aid thieves masquerading as colleges and universities, online courses will still be held in suspicion in many quarters of academe." Why would anyone—the argument goes—want to give up the personal and deep relationship one can cultivate with students in a physical classroom with the exploitative and isolating potential of online education? Comparing the two modalities of online education and face-to-face education is a natural tendency among many people—including students, researchers, policymakers, and laypeople. After all, if we want to offer the best education for our students, identifying which modality is "the best" will ultimately benefit them. But rather than try to answer the question of whether online education can ever be as good as face-to-face education, this chapter argues that one-to-one comparisons between face-to-face and online courses are ultimately unhelpful and that any course is only as good as its design and its ability to meet the needs of its students. In other words, "which one is better?" is the wrong question to ask.

When it comes to preferences between modalities, a recent survey of nearly 65,000 undergraduate students in the United States found that most students (55%) prefer a blended learning environment over purely face-to-face or online environments (Galanek, Gierdowski, and Brooks 2018). In probing these results further, the authors report that experience with and exposure to learning environments drive these preferences. They report that students "who have never taken a completely online class are significantly more likely to prefer face-to-face-only courses, and vice versa . . . students who have taken at least some of their courses online are significantly more likely to prefer blended environments and less likely to prefer purely face-to-face courses." A *preference* for a particular modality, however, does not necessarily mean that the modality will lead to superior learning outcomes compared to the alternatives.

One of the problems with debates comparing online to face-to-face courses is that some arguments tend to assume that face-to-face education is uniform and always effective, personal, and engaging. But surely most of us have taken courses that haven't always met that standard, courses in which we felt disengaged, our learning experience was generally poor, or the course objectives were not met. Many factors may have contributed to those outcomes, ranging from a problematic instructional design (e.g., a misalignment between learning objectives and assessments) to our own interest on the topic or the instructor's commitment to the course. Further, consider just how "personal" face-to-face learning typically is for a large class of perhaps 200 or even 400 students meeting in an auditorium. The most efficient and common way to teach such a class is through a series of lectures, but does that really make for a class that reflects individual students' needs, interests, and motivations? Now imagine an alternative instructional approach for this class that involves students' reading relevant literature prior to class, coming to class with questions, and, with guidance from the instructor, working in groups of four or five on activities aligned to the goals of the course and joining interest-based post-course labs to work on their assignments. Even though both courses occur in a face-to-face environment, the experiences of the students who take them would differ remarkably. The same is true of online courses. In short, modality doesn't mean uniformity, and, therefore, modality should not be the barometer by which we should judge the quality of courses.

The research on this issue is telling. While individual studies have occasionally reported findings that support one modality over the other, large-scale studies and meta-analyses have found little or no evidence that outcomes between online courses and face-to-face courses differ significantly (e.g., Bernard et al. 2004; Zhao et al. 2005). One of the best-known meta-analyses in this area, described in Means, Toyama, Murphy, and Baki (2013), found that even though learners in online courses performed modestly better than learners in face-to-face courses, there were no significant differences between the two modalities. The researchers did find significant differences in outcomes between blended and face-to-face conditions (higher outcomes in the former). However, they warn that these results should be interpreted with caution, as many studies didn't account for other variables (e.g., extra time on tasks, differences in pedagogy) that could affect the results. In other words, everything else being equal and as far as learning outcomes are concerned, we should expect no significant differences in student performance between online and face-to-face courses.

Everything else is never equal, however, which is why one-to-one comparisons between online and face-to-face courses tend to be misleading in the overwhelming majority of cases. Online education and face-to-face education lie on a continuum, along which lie courses that blend face-to-face and online components in different proportions. For example, some face-to-face courses may include online components in the form of readings, videos, and a/synchronous discussions hosted within a learning management system. Some online courses may invite students to meet with peers or others in face-to-face settings such as discipline conferences, and online degrees may include short-term, face-to-face residencies.

The human condition is perhaps the factor that makes comparative studies problematic: on any given day, students may be having a bad (or wonderful) day, facing an illness, or caring for an elderly parent. Or, they and their instructors, may be feeling generous or sad, sleep-deprived, or excited to study a topic that, for one reason or another, they find particularly meaningful.

Another problem with this debate is that it too often seems to imply that face-to-face education is somehow inherently "good" and that online education is inherently "bad." Some critics, for instance, suggest that a transition to online education will force educators to "surrender" their pedagogy "to corporate control, monetization or groupthink" (Mentz and Schaberg 2018). While such concerns are not unfounded, Ross and Bayne (2016) remind us that "online teaching need not be complicit with the instrumentalization of education" and can, in fact, be mobilized to resist such efforts, such as through designs that emphasize community-oriented approaches to learning. Clearly, the pressures on higher education to function as a commodity, compete on a global scale, treat students as consumers, and generally reflect a market ideology are not limited to just one mode of education. This recognition behooves us to consider whose power and privilege is perpetuated whenever a particular mode of learning is declared "the best," and to recognize that teaching face-to-face doesn't necessarily equate to resisting neoliberal pressures on higher education. We need to reframe this concern in terms of pedagogy: in what ways does the course pedagogy resist those pressures, regardless of modality? As Dr. Ross Perkins once noted, advocates for face-to-face education also need to acknowledge that in-person education tends to privilege particular students, such as those who have the means and support necessary to move and live far away from home (2019, personal conversation).

In sum, the larger issue behind this debate is what conditions make for a high-quality educational experience, one that is effective, efficient, engaging, socially just, and meaningful and isn't exploitative, unfair, or available only to those who can afford it. An online course may be as unaffordable as a face-to-face one, and a face-to-face course is as likely as an online course to perpetuate dangerous stereotypes and leave particular demographics of students behind. Ultimately, the value of an online course or degree rests upon its design and the strategies it employs rather than its modality.

···

- Physical copresence is not a prerequisite for a high-quality learning experience.
- The question of whether online learning is as good as or better than in-person, or face-to-face, learning is the wrong one to ask.
- Meta-analyses and systematic reviews of the literature have generally found no significant differences in learning outcomes between online and face-to-face settings.
- Courses can be problematic, commodifying, instrumental, and unjust regardless of their modality. To address such issues, examine particular designs and particular courses rather than modalities.

References
Bernard, R. M., Abrami, P. C., Lou, Y., Borokhovski, E., Wade, A., Wozney, L., Wallet, P. A., Fiset, M., and Huang, B. 2004. "How Does Distance Education Compare with Classroom Instruction? A Meta-analysis of the Empirical Literature." *Review of Educational Research* 74 (3): 379–439.

Galanek, J. D., Gierdowski, D. C., and Brooks, D. C. 2018. *ECAR Study of Undergraduate Students and Information Technology, 2018*. Boulder, CO: ECAR.

Gannon, K. 2019. "4 Lessons from Moving a Face-to-Face Course Online." *Chronicle Vitae*, March 25. https://chroniclevitae.com /news/2176-4-lessons-from-moving-a-face-to-face-course-online.

Jaschik, S., and Lederman, D. 2018. *2018 Survey of Faculty Attitudes on Technology*. Washington, DC: Inside Higher Education.

Means, B., Toyama, Y., Murphy, R., and Baki, M. 2013. "The Effectiveness of Online and Blended Learning: A Meta-Analysis of the Empirical Literature." *Teachers College Record* 115 (3): 1–47.

Mentz, S., and Schaberg, C. 2018. "Online Learning: A 2-Voiced Case for Ambivalence." *Inside Higher Ed*, December 4. https://www .insidehighered.com/views/2018/12/04/two-scholars-debate-pros -and-cons-online-learning-opinion.

Ross, J., and Bayne, S. 2016. "The Manifesto for Teaching Online." *University of Edinburgh* (blog). https://blogs.ed.ac.uk/manifesto teachingonline/the-text/.

Zhao, Y., Lei, J., Yan, B., Lai, C., and Tan, H. S. 2005. "What Makes the Difference? A Practical Analysis of Research on the Effectiveness of Distance Education." *Teachers College Record* 107 (8): 1836.

2.

The Learner Who Was "Nontraditional"

Peter is in his mid-thirties. He lives in an affluent country in Europe with his partner and two daughters and works full-time as a police officer. He regularly works 12-hour shifts, although the days of the week that he works change frequently. He enrolled in an online program offered by an open university located in a neighboring town to earn a certificate in legal and justice studies primarily because, he told me during a face-to-face interview, "I don't have time to go to a classroom." Even still, he reported, "I have to go to the university for the final exam for each class I take, and that's a real pain because I have to coordinate with work." Sensing that his coursework adds stress to Peter's life, I asked him to share with me the reasons he's pursuing this credential. "It's for promotion," he said; without it, he is stuck in his current position, unable to achieve his aspirations for a better future for himself and his family, as so many other coworkers with more connections, credentials, and degrees have done. For Peter, obtaining more education was essential to his career progression, and an online program that accommodated his work schedule was the only viable path he could find to achieve his goal.

In many ways, Peter's life and studies are a marked contrast to those of many other online students, such as the US student described by Cavanagh (2012, 215):

> Jennifer is a 20-year-old sophomore at a large state university. She lives in a dorm, works as a resident assistant, belongs to a sorority, works part time at a local hotel, and dances ballet.
> By all external measures, she is the typical "traditional" college student. Yet, within the past year, she has not only taken "traditional" face-to-face courses, but has also taken courses in what many might consider "nontraditional" modalities: both fully online and blended formats (blended learning mixes both online and face-to-face elements). And she is not alone.

Peter and Jennifer are at different ages in their life, living quite different lives in different parts of the world, but are attending online courses. These courses fit their individual circumstances, their lives and needs. Together, these two short stories illustrate a few of the ways in which both traditional and nontraditional students are being served by the rising prevalence of online and distance learning. It is, therefore, important to recognize that there is no single kind of online student, and simply designing online education for one uniformly imagined audience (e.g., mid-career working professionals, undergraduate students who work full-time, students in remote communities, midlife individuals who care for elderly parents) may do more harm than good. Put simply, many different people enroll in online learning.

•••

Although reliable data on trends in online education enrollments worldwide are difficult to come by, leading this chapter to focus largely on demographic data from North America, the global trend seems to be a growth in enrollments. In many areas of the world, such as Brazil, China, and Turkey, online and distance education enrollments have been growing rapidly largely to meet the increased demand for education at all levels. In some places, such as Australia, Canada, Germany, and the United States, they are growing steadily; while in others they are declining in response to broader sociocultural and economic forces, such as decreased funding for education in the United Kingdom or demographic declines in Russia (Zawacki-Richter and Qayyum 2019). If anything, the estimates of people who are learning online discussed in this chapter are conservative, as they do not reflect individuals enrolled in not-for-credit online courses or in online courses from non-university providers. They do not take into account, for instance, the more than 5.6 million learners who enrolled in MOOCs offered by Harvard and MIT alone between 2012 and 2018, or the more than 100 million individuals across the world who had signed up for at least one MOOC by 2018 (Class Central 2018; Nesterko et al. 2019). Even though there is some evidence that the demand for MOOCs may be unsustainable and declining (Reich and Ruipérez-Valiente 2019), the numbers cited below also do not reflect the vast number of people who go online daily to informally gain skills, competencies, and retrieve information on topics as specialized as particular philosophies of past centuries or as mundane as fixing a leaky faucet.

The data regarding enrollments in online higher education offerings in North America reported below come from three organizations: the US Education Department's National Center for Education Statistics; the Babson Survey Research Group, which, with a number of partners, conducts an annual survey of online education in the United States; and the recently established Canadian Digital Learning Research Association, which, so far, has conducted Canadian-focused surveys in 2017, 2018, and 2019. Whereas the US Department of Education tracks higher education data nationally, Canada does not have an equivalent federal body, which makes it more difficult to capture data on digital learning across the country.

In the United States, overall enrollment in online courses has increased steadily over the years. In 2000, only 6% of postsecondary students in the United States took at least one online course; by 2017, the latest data from the US Department of Education show, this percentage had risen to 33% (Ginder, Kelly-Reid, and Mann 2019). Of those enrolled in online education, 15.4% were enrolled exclusively in online courses and 17.6% were enrolled in a blend of online and face-to-face courses. Significantly, while overall enrollments in postsecondary education fell by about half a percent between 2000 and 2017, the number of students who took some of their courses online grew by nearly 6%—that is, by about the total percentage of students taking online courses in 2000. According to Seaman, Allen, and Seaman, this resulted in "over a million fewer students coming to campus in 2016 than there was in 2012" (2018, 24), a decline that has affected mostly private for-profit institutions. Even though the for-profit online education sector saw a surge in enrollments around 2008–2010, partly as a result of adult learners seeking to update their skills during a harsh economic downturn, since 2010 many not-for-profit online learning providers entered the market. As an examination of the enrollment trends at particular institutions reported in figure 1 reveals, many institutions have experienced significant enrollment shifts over the past few years: the for-profit University of Phoenix, for instance, has seen a steep decline in its enrollment, while Western Governors University and Southern New Hampshire University, both not-for-profit universities offering competency-based degrees, have seen a rapid growth in their numbers.

The picture is slightly different in Canada, which Jean-Louis (2015) describes as a hot spot for distance education. Canadian provinces offer many options, including blended and fully online options, to support their public undergraduate, graduate, and skills-based programs. Jean-Louis reported that the number of students registered online in Canada was more than 1.3 million, a number that, according to Bates (2018), has steadily grown. By now, nearly all public, Canadian, postsecondary institutions offer online courses, and many universities in Canada (like others in the United States and United Kingdom) have actively recruited international students, who pay higher tuition than domestic students for course offerings. Although almost all higher education subjects are available online, the most popular are offered in programs in business, education, and health, such as nursing. As the Canadian economy becomes increasingly dependent on highly educated knowledge workers, a postsecondary degree is becoming even more of a necessity (Contact North 2012). This recognition has led to an increased investment in postsecondary education and in online learning to accommodate nontraditional learners entering postsecondary education later in life. Nonetheless, Canada, like many other nations, still has a number of challenges to overcome if it is to make online learning as available and effective as advocates might like, including improving upon its quality, expanding affordable access to education, and reducing digital divides through expanding broadband access in northern communities.

2017 Rank	Institution (gray= for-profit)	DE 2012	DE 2013	DE 2014	DE 2015	DE 2016
1	University of Phoenix	251,148	206,737	198,088	169,955	134,678
2	Western Governors University	41,369	46,733	57,821	70,504	84,289
3	Southern New Hampshire University	10,679	20,701	35,861	53,760	61,495
4	Grand Canyon University	28,417	45,496	49,685	54,118	58,779
5	Liberty University	61,786	64,503	67,780	66,300	60,850
6	Walden University	50,209	51,016	52,188	52,799	52,565
7	University of Maryland-University College	36,072	33,873	39,482	41,898	44,308
8	American Public University System	58,115	55,422	57,539	52,361	48,623
9	Strayer University	24,426	21,549	24,806	29,847	33,984
10	Kaplan University	48,373	54,930	56,294	45,380	38,404
11	Ashford University	76,722	57,235	50,541	42,046	41,343
12	Capella University	35,754	34,007	35,061	34,365	37,569
13	Excelsior College	39,728	39,897	41,527	43,123	41,658
14	Brigham Young University-Idaho	6,139	11,562	20,071	25,352	25,820
15	Arizona State University	7,444	9,958	13,749	19,884	25,758
16	Chamberlain University	10,415	12,085	16,661	20,760	22,996
17	Colorado Technical University	24,819	22,738	23,041	24,174	24,132
18	DeVry University	44,625	36,413	32,877	28,890	25,048
19	Columbia Southern University	19,933	20,185	21,359	20,823	21,442
20	Ultimate Medical Academy	11,120	9,951	11,354	—	16,140
21	The University of Texas at Arlington	6,013	6,055	10,302	12,665	15,510
22	Pennsylvania State University	9,333	10,575	11,707	13,286	14,198
23	Ivy Tech Community College	15,513	16,493	15,809	13,989	14,296
24	Lone Star College System	7,428	7,308	8,859	8,640	9,166
25	Full Sail University	15,624	13,588	12,431	13,077	12,983
26	Colorado State University-Global Campus	5,258	7,402	9,259	9,838	11,605
27	Embry-Riddle Aeronautical University-Worldwide	9,726	9,393	10,928	11,274	11,632
28	Thomas Edison State University	20,456	20,739	21,341	13,009	12,441
29	National University	11,100	11,618	11,341	10,468	11,599
30	Northcentral University	9,252	10,928	11,160	11,029	10,916

DE 2017	2012-17 % DE Change	Trend	Current LMS
105,855	-58%		Homegrown > Bb Learn
98,627	138%		Homegrown
83,919	686%		D2L Brightspace
64,551	127%		LoudCloud Systems
59,840	-3%		Bb Learn
49,680	-1%		Bb Learn
46,736	30%		D2L Brightspace
46,420	-20%		Sakai
37,897	55%		Bb Learn
36,789	-24%		Bb Learn > D2L
36,452	-52%		Canvas
36,284	1%		Bb Learn
34,022	-14%		Canvas
31,554	414%		D2L > Canvas
30,583	311%		Bb Learn > Canvas
24,631	136%		Canvas
24,238	-2%		LoudCloud Systems
21,617	-52%		Canvas
20,818	4%		Bb Learn
18,345	65%		Bb Learn
16,532	175%		Bb Learn > Canvas
15,177	63%		Bb Learn > Canvas
13,369	-14%		Canvas
13,243	78%		D2L Brightspace
12,626	-19%		Moodle
12,381	135%		Schoology > Canvas
12,307	27%		Canvas
11,864	-42%		Moodle
11,746	6%		Moodle
10,788	17%		D2L Brightspace

Figure 1. Top 30 institutions by number of students taking at least one online course. DE = distance education. Reprinted by permission from https://mfeldstein .com/fall-2017-top-30-largest-online -enrollments-us/

Nontraditional learners present their own set of challenges for educators and institutions. The term *nontraditional student* is typically used to refer to learners who are considered independent for financial aid purposes, have one or more dependents, lack a traditional high school diploma, have delayed their postsecondary education, attend school part-time, or are employed full-time (Radford, Cominole, and Skomsvold 2015). Unlike conventional forms of education based on face-to-face, daytime courses, online learning is often able to accommodate and attract increasing numbers of working adults who support a family and seek a credential on a part-time basis, which is a reason that online learning is often seen solely as a kind of education for this group of students.

In the United States, the typical nontraditional undergraduate student is 32–34 years old, female, nonmilitary, US-based, employed full-time, and returning to school to attend health- or business-related programs (Friedman 2017). In 2016, approximately 3.5 million US students were pursuing online degrees, a number which is projected to increase to 5 million by 2020 as students are expected to continue opting for online learning as their modality of choice (Clinefelter and Aslanian 2016). Although nontraditional students taking online courses cite several motivations for continuing their education, their career aspirations tend to be most important, as in the case of Peter. According to Clinefelter and Aslanian, such students are particularly interested in a "speed to degree" option with "accelerated course offerings, year-round course scheduling, and a generous transfer credit policy," the latter mainly because 32% of US undergraduate students had dropped out of previous programs because of family or financial factors (26). Nonetheless, recent reports suggest that younger students are also increasingly enrolling in full-time online degree programs. By 2016, the average age of online college students had dropped to 29 for undergraduate online students and to 33 for graduate online students; online students were also more likely to be single, have fewer children, and earn less, with the percentage of graduate students earning less than $25,000 more than doubling since 2013.

Although many discussions on online learning focus on the technology and platforms that make it possible or stand to change its delivery, the data discussed in this chapter make clear that broader demographic trends are a force to be reckoned with, impacting not just enrollments but the ways that universities design and deliver their programs. A report by the New Media Consortium (2017) for instance warns that institutions which "do not already have robust strategies" for online learning "simply will not survive." I hold a slightly different perspective: Some institutions may not survive the pressures facing them, while others strategically employ online learning offerings and other innovations. Yet others, due to a wide variety of factors including prestige and access to large endowments, may employ digital learning with a sense of luxury, as an add-on perhaps, as a way to explore options, diversify, and reach new and different students.

...

- Online learning enrollments are generally growing but not everywhere and not uniformly.
- Nontraditional students comprise a sizable group of individuals pursuing online learning opportunities.
- Working adults, are a growing market opportunity, even though younger learners are also enrolling on online learning as well.

References

Bates, T. 2018. "The 2017 National Survey of Online Learning in Canadian Post-Secondary Education: Methodology and Results." *International Journal of Educational Technology in Higher Education* 15 (29): 2–17.

Cavanagh, T. B. 2012. "The Postmodality Era: How 'Online Learning' Is Becoming 'Learning.'" In *Game Changers: Education and Information Technology*, edited by D. Oblinger, 215–228. Boulder, CO: Educause.

Class Central. 2018. "By the Numbers: MOOCS in 2018." https://www.class-central.com/report/mooc-stats-2018/.

Clinefelter, D. L., and Aslanian, C. B. 2016. *Online College Students 2016: Comprehensive Data on Demands and Preferences.* Louisville, KY: Learning House.

Contact North. 2012. "Online Learning in Canada: At a Tipping Point." https://teachonline.ca/sites/default/files/pdf/innovation -practices/onlinelearningincanadareport_june_12_2012.pdf.

Friedman, J. 2017. "The Average Online Bachelor's Student." *U.S. News*, April 4. https://www.usnews.com/higher-education/online -education/articles/2017-04-04/us-news-data-the-average-online -bachelors-student.

Ginder, S. A., Kelly-Reid, J. E., and Mann, F. B. 2019. *Enrollment and Employees in Postsecondary Institutions, Fall 2017; and Financial Statistics and Academic Libraries, Fiscal Year 2017: First Look (Provisional Data).* NCES 2019-021. Washington, DC: National Center for Education Statistics.

Jean-Louis, M. 2015. *An Overview of Online Learning in Canada: Canada as a Hot Spot for Creative and Imaginative Developments in Open Distance Learning and Open Educational Resources.* Contact North, April. https://contactnorth.ca/sites/default/files/pdf /external-presentations/an_overview_of_online_learning_in _canada.pdf.

Nesterko, S. O., Seaton, D. T., Kashin, K., Han, Q., Reich, J., Waldo, J., Chuang I., and Ho, A. D. 2019. "World Map of Enrollment." *HarvardX Insights.* http://harvardx.harvard.edu/harvardx -insights/world-map-enrollment.

New Media Consortium. 2017. *Horizon Report: 2017 Higher Education Edition.* http://cdn.nmc.org/media/2017-nmc-horizon-report-he -EN.pdf.

Radford, A. W., Cominole, M., and Skomsvold, P. 2015. *Demographic and Enrollment Characteristics of Nontraditional Undergraduates:*

2011–12. Web Tables. NCES 2015-025. Washington, DC: National Center for Education Statistics. https://nces.ed.gov/pubsearch /pubsinfo.asp?pubid=2015025.

Reich, J., and Ruipérez-Valiente, J. A. 2019. "The MOOC Pivot." *Science* 363 (6423): 130–131.

Seaman, J. E., Allen, I. E., and Seaman, J. 2018. *Grade Increase: Tracking Distance Education in the United States.* Oakland, CA: Babson Survey Research Group. http://onlinelearningsurvey.com /reports/gradeincrease.pdf.

Zawacki-Richter, O., and Qayyum, A. 2019. *Open and Distance Education in Asia, Africa and the Middle East: National Perspectives in a Digital Age.* Singapore: Springer.

3.

The Learner Whose Motive
Was Sheer Interest

While I was arranging a phone interview with Laura, she mentioned that she would be in Belgium when we spoke. In fluent English, she told me that she was 29 years old and had graduated from medical school in 2016. "Since then, I've specialized in internal medicine and now in laboratory medicine. I've also worked a bit abroad with Doctors Without Borders, but now I'm back in Belgium, where I'm from."

At the time we spoke, Laura was enrolled in an online physics course. I was interested in learning what she felt that physics had to do with medicine at this stage in her life, and she was quick to explain what had motivated her to enroll in this course:

> I never studied physics or anything like that, but I've always
> had an interest in the more philosophical aspects of physics,
> like quantum theory and relativity theory. But because I'd
> never really taken any courses on it, I did read some popular
> scientific books, where they tried to explain it for people who
> have not studied anything like that and with not too much math

in it. So, when I saw the course, I thought it might be something that I would be interested in, so that's why I decided to take it.

Though Laura admitted to being "a bit behind" in her studies—like many people, she was busy with work and didn't have enough time to accomplish everything on her plate—she was motivated to finish the course. In fact, she was enrolled in multiple courses, some more interesting and pressing than others: while the physics course was purely interest-driven, others were more directly related to her professional aspirations.

...

Why do people choose to take online courses? Some people may be deeply embedded in online environments and find online education a perfectly natural and worthwhile option; others may approach online education with greater trepidation and skepticism. Some individuals may view the internet as a crucial component of their life and treat it as inextricably linked to their identity. If online banking is perfectly acceptable to such people, why wouldn't online courses? Other people see the internet as a tool that serves particular functions on an as-needed basis and may view online courses as instrumental options for particular needs. Yet others might have more anxiety about online learning but for whom, despite their convictions or doubts, online education may be the only option available.

The motivations of students who choose to engage in online learning vary between intrinsic and extrinsic, which in turn may vary across student populations and affect a student's choice about whether to go fully online or stay on campus and take some of their courses online. As Hartnett, George, and Dron (2011) revealed in their study based on self-determination theory, students' motivations for engaging in online learning tend to be situated, as in Laura's case, suggesting that "individuals can be motivated to a greater or lesser degree, and in different ways, in any given context and time" (22).

We know that some students choose online learning specifically for the autonomy it affords them. The ability to learn online can be tailored to individuals' unique life situations and provide them access to education and credentials that would otherwise be out of their reach for a wide range of reasons, such as geography, employment, or family obligations. Students are forthcoming about these reasons. One blogger quoted in *Times Higher Education* cited both intrinsic and extrinsic reasons for choosing to study online while working full time. "Online learning enabled me to hone skills such as self-motivation and time management that ultimately made me a better student, and later, a more prepared young adult," she claimed, and "learning on my own enabled me to craft an education that was unique to me" (Stauffer 2018). Such agency, she argued, has become increasingly important to today's students: "As the world changes rapidly and the workforce evolves with it, options like online learning create opportunity for students to take charge of what their learning and life will look like," because "students in the US and UK want more flexibility than ever from their education," she predicted, "gone are the days of a 'typical' university experience."

Employment is another strong motivator for many students. In a study of mature nontraditional students in Australia, Stone, O'Shea, May, Delahunty, and Partington (2016) found that participants used their access to Australia's Open University online as an opportunity to improve their careers. The researchers reported that "without the opportunity to study online many of these students indicate that they would not be studying at all," as it was "only due to the availability and flexibility of online study that they [felt] able to embark on this journey" (162). Most of Stone et al.'s participants were women with children and working full-time, and thus access to online education was a viable and fitting way to gain new or better skills and improve their future work possibilities. These students, most of whom were the first in their families to attend postsecondary education, were highly motivated to succeed and access career progression and employment opportunities that would improve the lives of their families.

In a case study of similar students by Henry, Pooley, and Omari (2014), the motivating factors behind seeking online learning opportunities were convenience, flexibility, accessibility, the attraction to a specific course or institution, the benefits of a university education, and extrinsic encouragement from a significant other or employer. Most of the online learners in this study were women with children who were pursuing a bachelor's degree in health or business and were new to online learning. Citing convenience and flexibility, these participants "were of the opinion that studying online would facilitate more time, place and pace flexibility, allowing more time to attend to family responsibilities and/or maintain students' desired employment arrangements while pursuing university studies, than would an on-campus course" (4). This finding is also supported by Ruffalo Noel Levitz (2017), whose *National Student Satisfaction and Priorities Report* concluded that online learners' motivations were "convenience, work schedule, [and] flexible pacing for completing the program" and that online learning "is all about convenience and balancing course work with life's other demands" (17). Accessibility was especially critical for students with disabilities, for whom online learning allowed them to bypass physical barriers to attending classes on-site. Students also reported choosing a particular institution because of its fit with their possible future employment needs and selecting a campus closer to home in order to "feel more connected with the program or in case they needed to visit the campus" (5). In a study of mature online students, Harris and Martin (2012) found that the largest number were women and that work, family, living away from the campus, and the convenience and flexibility of completing online work when it suited their schedule were their primary motivating factors.

Two additional factors that are reported as motivating students to take online courses are cost efficiencies (e.g., Jaggers 2014) and discomfort with the traditional campus environment (e.g., Fox 2017). The cost of attending college invariably impacts student choice. Online options may eliminate commuting and relocation costs, though such costs may also be minimized when learners enroll in face-to-face courses/programs closer to home. In their comparison on community college and for-profit enrollments, Iloh and Tierney (2014) illustrate how the cost-benefit analysis that students engage in when selecting institutions is more complicated than merely selecting a low-cost option. For instance, they find that some students select higher-cost colleges as they might perceive higher long-term benefits arising from those options. In a study by Fox (2017), avoiding possible negative interactions contributed to participants' choosing to engage in online learning, particularly among mature students and parents: "Students expressed a desire to avoid being judged by students and instructors and described the classroom space as involving a lot of pressure and being intimidating" (5). One of Fox's participants for example, described online courses as "'intellectually pure spaces' in which students are not judged based on gender, age, race, sexuality, religion, etc." (5).

Motivations for participating in other kinds of online learning experiences tend to be similar. Kizilcec and Schneider (2015), for instance, reported that among students' motivating factors for enrolling in a MOOC were "to earn a certificate, to improve English skills, and a variety of social, academic, vocational, and interest-driven motivations" (16). Yet, contextual factors matter, as the study by Hartnett, George, and Dron (2011) I noted earlier indicated, and should be taken into consideration. For instance, Kizilcec and Schneider found that if a MOOC was related to a students' academic pursuits, students also used the MOOCs as a reference tool—as a way of gaining access to the resources used within the course.

Although many on-campus students are also choosing to take online courses for their flexibility and convenience, the motivations of these students, who are in general younger and without children, tend to be somewhat different than those exclusively online or more mature students. Some of the factors that on-campus students cite for enrolling in online classes include the ability to take a course at a convenient time or that was not currently available on campus, to avoid large lecture hall classes, to earn additional credits, to gain access to specific faculty members who only teach online, and to fit a personal preference for online learning. The Education Advisory Board (2017) also reported that, like Jennifer in chapter 2, many on-campus students were heavily involved in campus life activities and in working part-time and therefore also desired the flexibility that online courses can afford.

Recognizing the range of learners' motivations to pursue online options is helpful because these motivations may impact participation, achievement, and potentially the design of online courses. For instance, learners who join an online class to explore a topic or to consider the discipline as a major are likely to show different participation patterns than learners who enroll in the same course because it satisfies a requirement for graduation or because it is a free online course that allows them to dip their toes into a topic. While in some instances students may have limited options (e.g., in their desire to pursue a unique program that is offered in one particular modality), in most cases students make decisions based upon a variety of factors, ranging from the cost of a program, to the reputation of the institution, to the anticipated benefits that they will accrue from further education.

...

- Students enroll in online learning offerings for a wide variety of reasons ranging from financial concerns, to convenience, to feelings of connectedness with a particular university.

References

Education Advisory Board. 2017. "Why Would an On-Campus Student Take Online Classes?" https://www.eab.com/daily -briefing/2017/03/27/why-would-an-on-campus-student-take -online-classes.

Fox, H. L. 2017. "What Motivates Community College Students to Enroll Online and Why It Matters." *Insights on Equity and Outcomes* 19 (January): 1–11.

Harris, H. S., and Martin, E. W. 2012. "Student Motivations for Choosing Online Classes." *International Journal for the Scholarship of Teaching and Learning* 6 (2): 1–8. https://digitalcommons .georgiasouthern.edu/cgi/viewcontent.cgi?article=1342&context =ij-sotl.

Hartnett, M., George, A. S., and Dron, J. 2011. "Examining Motivation in Online Distance Learning Environments: Complex, Multifaceted and Situation-Dependent." *International Review of Research in Open and Distributed Learning* 12 (6): 20–38.

Henry, M. K., Pooley, J. A., and Omari, M. 2014. "Student Motivations for Studying Online: A Qualitative Study." *Proceedings of the Teaching and Learning Forum.* https://ro.ecu.edu.au/cgi/view content.cgi?article=1870&context=ecuworkspost2013.

Iloh, C., and Tierney, W. G. 2014. "Understanding For-Profit College and Community College Choice through Rational Choice." *Teachers College Record* 116 (8): 1–34.

Jaggers, S. S. 2014. "Choosing between Online and Face-to-Face Courses: Community College Student Voices." *American Journal of Distance Education* 28 (1): 27–38.

Kizilcec, R. F., and Schneider, E. 2015. "Motivation as a Lens to Understand Online Learners: Toward Data-Driven Design with the OLEI Scale." *ACM Transactions on Computer-Human Interaction (TOCHI)* 22 (2): 6.

Ruffalo Noel Levitz. 2017. *2017 National Student Satisfaction and Priorities Report.* Cedar Rapids, IA: Ruffalo Noel Levitz. http://learn.ruffalonl.com/rs/395-EOG-977/images/2017_National_Student_Satisfaction_Report_1.0.pdf.

Stauffer, R. 2018. "The Real Experience of an Online-Only University Student." *Times Higher Education*, January 19. https://www.timeshighereducation.com/student/blogs/real-experience-online-only-university-student.

Stone, C., O'Shea, S., May, J., Delahunty, J., and Partington, Z. 2016. "Opportunity through Online Learning: Experiences of First-in-Family Students in Online Open-Entry Higher Education." *Australian Journal of Adult Learning* 56 (2): 146–169.

4.

The Learner Who Dropped Out

"I'm leaving my PhD program," James told me in a low voice.

I had spoken to James multiple times and found him sharp, funny, and meticulous. The last time I had talked to him, even though he had expressed some qualms about his studies, he had been eager to complete his PhD and was exploring potential faculty jobs even though his anticipated completion date was a couple of years away.

"What happened?" I asked.

"The pay is horrible, for one. I could be making a lot more as is without being at school, and once I'm out, it's not like I'll be making much more. I thought I enjoyed doing research, but I don't enjoy it *that* much."

James had the qualities to be an exceptional faculty member. He was always pleasant and wanted to make me feel comfortable. I was certain he would bring that kind of care to his classroom, and, for a moment, I felt sad about this missed opportunity for him and his potential students. I recognized that the pay for faculty positions in his discipline compared to the private sector is low and the financial and emotional costs of a degree are onerous—perhaps even more so than James was letting me in on—but I couldn't help but enjoy thinking of James leading a university classroom. He used to be a K–12 teacher, and from what I understood, his students had loved him.

"Anyway, I am not leaving the field," he continued. "On the way to the PhD, I picked up a few skills that I think I can apply to jobs in instructional design. There's plenty of companies around here looking for trainers, designers, and so on."

Did I mention that James was perceptive? It was as if he had read my mind and was trying to reassure me that the online courses he had taken had not been a waste.

···

While many students choose to learn online for a variety of reasons and successfully complete their programs online, attrition (or withdrawal or dropping out) is an issue that has long plagued distance education and online learning. It is important for faculty, administrators, and designers to understand why some students who are initially motivated to pursue an online education fail to complete a program while others continue to persist. Understanding the reasons behind persistence, attrition, and non-completion may help us understand our students better *and* develop solutions to address them.

Though participation in online learning continues to rise, postsecondary institutions still face the challenge of attrition and drop out within courses and programs. According to Croxton (2014), attrition rates for online courses range from 10% to as high as 75%. Many of the same work, family, and personal factors that motivate learners to enroll in online courses can also influence their decision to drop out. Limited academic support and financial challenges can also lead students to withdraw from a course or program (Beer and Lawson 2017).

According to Beer and Lawson, attrition is "a complex, non-linear problem" with an "interconnectivity of factors that contribute to the student's decision to leave" (780), leading these researchers to urge institutions to engage in collaborative, innovative, and learning-focused strategies to address the problem effectively.

Lee and Choi (2011) have identified three categories of factors contributing to attrition and dropping out: student factors, course and program factors, and environmental factors. These findings reaffirm prior research in in-person and distance education highlighting that students, like James who is concerned about the financial implications of his degree, face a complex combination of internal and external factors that impact their success (e.g., Aragon and Johnson 2008; Kember 1989; Sheets 1992; Tinto 1975). Lee and Choi report that students with less previous academic experience, weaker time-management and problem-solving skills, and lower technological skills were more likely to drop out than students with higher academic and technological skills whose internal locus of control allowed them to work through to completion of an online course. In terms of course design, well-designed programs offering institutional support and interaction reduced attrition, as did designs that encouraged active course participation. Environmental factors that increased students' persistence in a course or program included a supportive study environment (including financial and emotional support from work, family, friends, and the institution). Therefore, according to these authors, reducing dropout and attrition rates requires an "understanding of each student's challenges and potential, providing quality course activities and well-structured supports, and handling environmental issues and emotional challenges" (610). In other words, addressing dropout and attrition rates requires ecological interventions that target not only what students should or shouldn't be doing, but also what other actors could or shouldn't be doing, including the institution, the students' employers, and their family and friends.

This is a point that I will return to multiple times throughout the book. Significantly, the majority of the literature in the area imagines students as being autonomous and independent, so much so that individual actions are often seen as capable of resolving the challenges students may be facing. While that may be true in some cases, and indeed some personal steps may help learners address challenges—such as, for example, the recommendation to reduce distractions while studying—we should recognize that individual effort and personal responsibility can only go so far in an environment where institutional, familial, and societal supports may be lacking.

Bawa (2016) for example, points out that students who are new to online education may be surprised by the time commitment and rigor of online courses, and find that meeting the demands of such courses may require a new level of academic time management and discipline. Bawa notes that "if learners are not comfortable with self-learning and constructing knowledge out of their own initiatives, the online environment can become intimidating for them" (4), and thus helping students develop self-directed learning skills can positively affect their motivation to continue within a course. However, such personal action may need to be accompanied by broader support including instructional scaffolds, institutional supports, familial support, and so on.

Other scholars have addressed this issue by examining factors that can increase student persistence. As Shaw, Burrus, and Ferguson (2016) argue, "effective online learning is about providing students with a rich, engaging, professionally-relevant, and academically rigorous education" (212), a point which affirms that attrition is related to the design of online learning experiences and not just students' readiness, family and job responsibilities, and other factors that they bring with them to postsecondary education. According to Kim and Frick (2011), persistence, as a "continuation of one's studies in spite of obstacles, is often considered a measure of program effectiveness by higher education institutions" (1) and is affected by "external factors such as course factors and support, person factors such as self-efficacy and autonomy, and academic factors such as time and study management" (22).

Some facilitators of persistence identified by Hart (2012) in a review of the literature included previous academic proficiency; intrinsic motivations, such as goals, self-efficacy, and relevance; satisfaction with a course or program due to high-quality interactions with instructors and peers; and support from family, friends, and coworkers. Identified barriers to persistence included a lack of academic and technological skills, limited external sources of support, and limited support and interaction with the instructor. Ultimately, according to Hart, an "almost unanimous agreement exists in the literature that communication with the instructor, motivation, and peer and family support can be used to overcome barriers to persistence and lead the student to success in an online course" (38). Croxton (2014) has also argued that course designs that foster interactions between students and their instructors and peers can play a significant role in the retention and persistence of online learners.

A practical approach to address the multidimensional nature of attrition, retention, and ultimately success in online settings requires investments in instructional design, learner support structures, and personalized interventions. This approach addresses individual, institutional, and environmental factors and may involve a wide-range of strategies ranging from institutions developing a sense of community among learners; instructors developing content that is relevant, useful, and interesting; and instructors identifying at-risk students early and intervening with appropriate supports or solutions. These suggestions acknowledge that, as Yang, Baldwin, and Snelson (2017) put it, "the quality of an online program seems to be an important factor that impacts students' persistence" (24) and recognize that attrition is impacted by an ecology of factors that go beyond the individual student. To foster persistence and success, high-quality online courses and programs must go beyond the learner. They must respond to the learners *and* their environment.

It is worth acknowledging that much has been said about high dropout rates in MOOCs. In studying ways that learners attempted to address challenges they faced in MOOCs, my colleagues and I arrived at the realization that non-completion may indicate something else, perhaps something instructive for typical higher education offerings. Following an investigation of nearly 100 learners' experiences in MOOCs, we wrote:

> From one perspective, students are signing up for multiple MOOCs and failing to complete some of them. From another perspective, MOOC students are inventing a much more dynamic course sampling and trial experience than what traditional residential "shopping periods" allow. Rather than committing to a set of learning experiences by an arbitrary date, participants dynamically allocate their attention and effort as they are able and in courses that prove capable of capturing their interest.

Rather than ask the question "Why can't MOOC providers motivate students to make the same commitments that traditional higher education requires of course registrants?" it might be equally productive to ask, "Why can't traditional educational offerings adjust to allow students to make the kinds of flexible allocation of learning time and commitment that MOOC students are demonstrating?" While it makes sense for faculty to consider how they can reduce attrition within their own courses, it is also important to recognize that dropping a course can be a signal of a deepening commitment to another course. (Veletsianos, Reich, and Pasquini 2016, 8)

•••

- Dropout and attrition are one of the most significant challenges facing online learners.
- Dropout and attrition are complex problems stemming from student factors (e.g., lack of preparation), course program factors (e.g., lack of interaction at the course level or lack of community at the program level), and broader environmental factors (e.g., lack of community/societal support).
- Addressing these problems requires an ecological approach that not only tackles individuals' circumstances and challenges but also targets systemic issues that contribute to student persistence or lack thereof. Solutions must respond to individual learners *and* their environments.

References

Aragon, S. R., and Johnson, E. S. 2008. "Factors Influencing Completion and Noncompletion of Community College Online Courses." *American Journal of Distance Education* 22 (3): 146–158.

Bawa, P. 2016. "Retention in Online Courses: Exploring Issues and Solutions—a Literature Review." *Sage Open* 6 (1): 1–11.

Beer, C., and Lawson, C. 2017. "The Problem of Student Attrition in Higher Education: An Alternative Perspective." *Journal of Further and Higher Education* 41 (6): 773-784.

Croxton, R. A. 2014. "The Role of Interactivity in Student Satisfaction and Persistence in Online Learning." *Journal of Online Learning and Teaching* 10 (2): 314.

Hart, C. 2012. "Factors Associated with Student Persistence in an Online Program of Study: A Review of the Literature." *Journal of Interactive Online Learning* 11 (1).

Kember, D. 1989. "A Longitudinal-Process Model of Drop-Out from Distance Education." *Journal of Higher Education* 60 (3): 278-301.

Kim, K. J., and Frick, T. W. 2011. "Changes in Student Motivation during Online Learning." *Journal of Educational Computing Research* 44 (1): 1-23.

Lee, Y., and Choi, J. 2011. "A Review of Online Course Dropout Research: Implications for Practice and Future Research." *Educational Technology Research and Development* 59 (5): 593-618.

Sheets, M. F. 1992. "Characteristics of Adult Education Students and Factors Which Determine Course Completion: A Review." *New Horizons in Adult Education and Human Resource Development* 6 (1): 3-18.

Shaw, M., Burrus, S., and Ferguson, K. 2016. "Factors that Influence Student Attrition in Online Courses." *Online Journal of Distance Learning Administration* 19 (3): 211-231.

Tinto, V. 1975. "Dropout from Higher Education: A Theoretical Synthesis of Recent Research." *Review of Educational Research* 45 (1): 89-125.

Veletsianos, G., Reich, J., and Pasquini, L. A. 2016. "The Life between Big Data Log Events: Learners' Strategies to Overcome Challenges in MOOCs." *AERA Open* 2 (3). https://doi.org/10.1177/2332858416657002.

Yang, D., Baldwin, S., and Snelson, C. 2017. "Persistence Factors Revealed: Students' Reflections on Completing a Fully Online Program." *Distance Education* 38 (1): 23-36.

5.

The Learner Who Used
the Family Computer

When I interviewed Mark, he described in detail how his schedule dictated his studies. In particular, he would log onto his class early every morning while his daughter was still asleep. Mark lived in Panama and had elected to homeschool his daughter after they moved there. Once his daughter woke up in the morning, she needed to use the only computer in the household to do her own schoolwork. Shared resources—in this case, the computer—necessitated this scheduling. "This morning," he reported, "I got up around 5:30 and made coffee, went to a small spare bedroom that we use as a study room, started up the computer, and worked on the course until maybe about 6:00." His daughter had priority "access to the machine," and he was second, using it "whenever it's free." His participation in online courses was thus shaped by economic, temporal, and geographic factors, as well as by the needs of his family, all of which influenced his educational experiences and potentially his success. His daughter's education was shaped by these factors in similar ways.

Mark was enthusiastic about his online courses. He felt that "democratization of education is really, really, really important, especially for, well, for everybody," but particularly important "for places like where I live." For Mark, and students like him, online education can provide access and opportunities that were unavailable in the past. Yet such access may still be unequal: neither he nor his daughter had unfettered access to devices, and their internet speed was slower than that available elsewhere. Nonetheless, he was grateful for the opportunity to enroll, participate, and pursue higher learning.

...

Paradoxical research findings can often lead us to question long-held assumptions. In one such set of research findings regarding community college learners, Xu and Jaggars (2013) found that students performed more poorly (lower grades, lower completion rates) online than in face-to-face courses, while Shea and Bidjerano (2014) found that students who took some of their courses online were more likely to obtain a credential than those who did not. In other words, despite students' earning lower grades and dropping out of online courses at higher rates than when taking face-to-face courses, those who take online courses complete degrees at greater rates. As Shea put it, students taking online courses appear to be "doing worse at the course level, but at the program level—despite lower grades—they're finishing" (Barshay 2015, para. 3).

So, what gives? We've already examined the factors that might explain the higher dropout and attrition rates in online courses, but what factors might help explain the higher degree completion rates? One might be the ease of enrollment: it may be easier for students to get into online courses than in-person ones, especially if a particular in-person course is not taught in a given term, generates more student interest than available seats, or satisfies a variety of requirements for majors and nonmajors alike (e.g., introductory social science courses). As Johnson and Mejia (2014) noted, "If a student's choice is between taking an online course or waiting for the course to be offered in a classroom at a convenient time, taking the online course can help expedite completion or transfer" (11) and thus allow students to complete their programs more quickly and easily. A second likely reason is that the flexibility of individual online courses may better accommodate students' professional and personal demands, especially those of nontraditional students, and make it more possible for students to complete their courses. Online learning, therefore, can become a pathway for learners with restricted access to face-to-face courses to nonetheless complete their degrees. More recent research by Shea and Bidjerano (2016) seems to support these findings, as does a study by James, Swan, and Daston (2016). The latter study examined retention rates of more than 650,000 students divided in three groups: those taking only face-to-face courses, those taking only online courses, and those taking some face-to-face and some online courses. Researchers found no differences in retention between the different groups, leading them to argue that "despite media reports to the contrary, taking online courses is not necessarily harmful to students' chances of being retained, and may provide course-taking opportunities that otherwise might not be available, especially for nontraditional students" (75).

Although access to online courses appears to support retention, researchers warn that increased access to online learning has not eliminated, and may even exacerbate, a variety of inequities. If access is not synonymous with success, what else might explain the fact that some online learners are successful and some are not? What might explain disparities among online learners? Understanding disparities between learners requires us to come to terms with what researchers have described as a *digital divide*, a term which is used to describe inequities between those who have access to technology and those who do not. As Wiburg (2003) observes, the digital divide reflects *a set of divides* resulting from economic, racial, gender, geographic, and other inequities. A common misconception is that digital divides merely reflect gaps resulting from access to technology—that is, gaps between those who have access to technology and those that do not—but the divides run deeper than that. Mark and his daughter may have access to technology but lack broadband access that might afford them the ability to engage in richer learning experiences. A second divide that separates this family from others is that of socioeconomic status: Mark has the skills, literacies, and financial means to be present in and supportive of his daughter's homeschooling and educational endeavors, while other parents may not. In other words, digital divides reflect structural inequities.

Much of the research on digital divides in education has been conducted in the K–12 context and has shown that children from higher socioeconomic groups have greater access to technology and to the internet outside of school than their counterparts. In particular, Goode (2010) showed that white, upper-class boys had more access to technology at home than students in low socioeconomic and high minority communities, who had less internet access in the home and attended schools with limited resources, where their teachers also had not been trained to teach effectively with technology. That the resulting differences in the educational outcomes of these two groups was not simply one of access to technology is supported by Warschauer's (2003) finding that it is the *use* of technology at both school and the home, not just access to it, that makes the digital divide between students significant. According to his results, K–12 students "who enjoy a high socioeconomic status more frequently use computers for experimentation, research and critical inquiry, whereas poor students engage in less challenging drills and exercises that do not take full advantage of computer technology" (47). According to Warschauer, these findings debunk technological determinism, the belief that simply putting technology—the equipment—in front of students is enough to alleviate the digital divide. Cuban's (1986) research in the use of technology in K–12 classrooms similarly showed that access to technology is rarely an equalizing force. Without attention to systemic issues of racism, sexism, and socioeconomic disparities and to pedagogy and instruction that uses technology in a more effective and fulsome way; simply expanding access to technology will do little for equity, will do little to close the digital divide.

Among the many implications of such findings for those designing online learning at the postsecondary level is that many students of color and lower socioeconomic status may not be prepared for college-level courses offered in an online setting. Though Johnson and Mejia (2014) reported that access to higher education through online learning has increased among some minority groups, such as African American students, they also found that "online learning exacerbates existing achievement gaps" between some minority groups and majority students (10). The study by Xu and Jaggars (2013) that found that students' performance was worse in online than face-to-face courses also found that "younger students, African Americans, Latinos, males, students with lower levels of academic skill, and part-time students are all likely to perform markedly worse in online courses than in traditional ones" (9). As a result, they warned, the "continued expansion of online learning could strengthen, rather than ameliorate, educational inequity" (23).

In short, although proponents have often characterized online learning platforms as democratizing forces that will enable broad access to education (Veletsianos and Moe 2017), access and success may also reflect and perpetuate a number of inequities. Creating more egalitarian structures in education, therefore, will require more than using new technologies to expand access to educational content. The story of MOOCs offers an instructive example of what can happen when we ignore the many socioeconomic, cultural, and political aspects that influence the use and adoption of online learning. One of the most problematic features of MOOCs is their potential to act as vehicles for digital neocolonialism, propagating western ideologies, ways of thought, and morals to diverse populations globally (Adam 2019). Early proponents of MOOCs heralded them as increasing access to educational opportunities for people with otherwise limited access. Yet, Jaggars (2014, para. 15) prophetically cautioned that while "MOOCs might indeed improve access to college-level learning among technology-savvy working adults who hope to upgrade their skills," there was little available evidence "that such methods of delivery will improve both access and success among other traditionally underserved populations." And indeed, research has confirmed that affluent learners with previous higher education experience have had greater success with MOOCs than less affluent learners with less education (Hansen and Reich 2015; Kizilcec and Halawa 2015).

Understanding that technology, and access to it, does not bridge digital divides is important because it follows that institutions need to find other ways to rectify inequities and expand educational opportunity and success. Paying more attention to the circumstances and needs of individual students may offer recourse to this problem. For instance, Bawa (2016) proposed that institutions could improve retention rates by offering orientation programs to prepare students and faculty for online learning, given that one major factor contributing to attrition in such courses is "the over-estimation of student capabilities with respect to the demands of time, commitment, and technological skills required in online learning" (7). Cultural diversity is another factor to consider when attempting to improve equity in access to and success. As Smith and Ayers (2006) have noted, "Technologically mediated learning experiences may accommodate the singularities of a dominant Western culture at the expense of cultural responsiveness to the cultural backgrounds of all participants" (401) and thereby unwittingly marginalize the very students they often claim to serve. Warschauer (2003) has also cautioned that technology should not be inserted into education without acknowledging that "it is woven into social systems and processes" and recognizing that "from a policy standpoint, the goal of bringing technology to marginalized groups is not merely to overcome a technological divide but instead to further a process of social inclusion" (47).

The literature on distance and online education is replete with recommendations on ways to improve it, ranging from recognizing that some students may be more adept at online learning than others (e.g., Zhao, Lei, Yan, Lai, and Tan 2005) to fostering social interactions between students and instructors (Bawa 2016). Perhaps the major lesson here, however, is that a variety of factors play into success in online learning and that access alone is not sufficient to ensure that online learners will be successful. A social justice orientation requires that educators, researchers, and institutions identify and peel away the multitude of barriers that can impact success in online learning.

...

- While some research shows that student performance in online courses is generally poorer than in-person courses, other research indicates that students who take some courses online may complete their degrees at higher rates than if they were solely taking face-to-face courses. Why?
  - o It may be easier to enroll in online courses.
  - o Online courses may be more flexible and accommodating.
- Greater access to online learning though has not eliminated inequities—it might even exacerbate them.
- Digital divides reflect structural inequities and may (1) help explain disparities in educational outcomes, and (2) illuminate why techno-deterministic approaches may be inadequate in bridging gaps between different groups of learners.

References

Adam, T. 2019. "Digital Neocolonialism and Massive Open Online Courses (MOOCs): Colonial Pasts and Neoliberal Futures." *Learning, Media and Technology* 43 (3): 365–380.

Barshay, J. 2015. "The Online Paradox at Community Colleges." *The Hechinger Report*, May 11. https://hechingerreport.org/the-online -paradox-at-community-colleges/.

Bawa, P. 2016. "Retention in Online Courses: Exploring Issues and Solutions—a Literature Review." *Sage Open* 6 (1): 1–11.

Cuban, L. 1986. *Teachers and Machines: The Classroom Use of Technology since 1920*. New York: Teachers College Press.

Goode, J. 2010. "The Digital Identity Divide: How Technology Knowledge Impacts College Students." *New Media & Society* 12 (3): 497–513.

Hansen, J. D., and Reich, J. 2015. "Democratizing Education? Examining Access and Usage Patterns in Massive Open Online Courses." *Science* 350 (6265): 1245–1248.

Jaggars, S. S. 2014. "Democratization of Education for Whom? Online Learning and Educational Equity." *Diversity and Democracy* 17 (1 Winter). http://www.aacu.org/diversitydemocracy/2014/winter/jaggars.

James, S., Swan, K., and Daston, C. 2016. "Retention, Progression and the Taking of Online Courses." *Online Learning* 20 (2): 75–96.

Johnson, H. P., and Mejia, M. C. 2014. "Online Learning and Student Outcomes in California's Community Colleges." *Public Policy Institute of California*. https://www.ppic.org/content/pubs/report/R_514HJR.pdf.

Kizilcec, R. F., and Halawa, S. 2015. "Attrition and Achievement Gaps in Online Learning." In *Proceedings of the Second (2015) ACM Conference on Learning @ Scale*, 57–66. New York: ACM. doi:10.1145/2724660.2724680.

Shea, P., and Bidjerano, T. 2014. "Does Online Learning Impede Degree Completion? A National Study of Community College Students." *Computers & Education* 75: 103–111.

Shea, P., and Bidjerano, T. 2016. "A National Study of Differences between Online and Classroom-Only Community College Students in Time to First Associate Degree Attainment, Transfer, and Dropout." *Online Learning* 20 (3): 14–15.

Smith, D. R., and Ayers, D. F. 2006. "Culturally Responsive Pedagogy and Online Learning: Implications for the Globalized Community College." *Community College Journal of Research and Practice* 30 (5–6): 401–415.

Veletsianos, G., and Moe, R. 2017. "The Rise of Educational Technology as a Sociocultural and Ideological Phenomenon." *Educause Review*. http://er.educause.edu/articles/2017/4/the-rise-of-educational-technology-as-a-sociocultural-and-ideological-phenomenon.

Warschauer, M. 2003. "Demystifying the Digital Divide: The Simple Binary Notion of Technology Haves and Have-Nots Doesn't Quite Compute." *Scientific American* 289 (2): 42–47.

Wiburg, K. 2003. "Technology and the New Meaning of Educational Equity." *Computers in the Schools* 20 (1/2): 113–128.

Xu, D., and Jaggars, S. S. 2013. *Adaptability to Online Learning: Differences across Types of Students and Academic Subject Areas.*

CCRC Working Paper No. 54. New York: Columbia University, Teachers College, Community College Research Center.

Zhao, Y., Lei, J., Yan, B., Lai, C., and Tan, H. S. 2005. "What Makes the Difference? A Practical Analysis of Research on the Effectiveness of Distance Education." *Teachers College Record* 107 (8): 1836–1884.

6.

The Learner Who Had the Necessary Literacies

The tweed jacket, bow tie, and graying hair of the learner on the other end of my research assistant's webcam presented the quintessential image of a professor. Graham was indeed a professor; he had spent the previous 30 years researching higher education policy at a prominent British university. It wasn't until 2012, after learning about MOOCs from articles in the mass media, that he took his first online course.

Although it had been quite a while since he had enrolled in a course as a student, Graham spoke enthusiastically about this course, a MOOC called "E-Learning and Digital Cultures" from the University of Edinburgh. "It was really massive— about 34,000 people. That was the first time I'd done any on-line course, so it was pretty overwhelming and exciting because I just didn't know about this kind of thing. It was a massive learning curve, and it was tremendous fun. It really was a hoot." Unlike the typical face-to-face or online courses that rely on lectures and instructors presenting information, this one used instructor-provided resources as jumping-off points for conversations among peers that took place across a number of online spaces. In addition to learning about the topic, Graham was learning how to use a number of technologies to interact with others. He reported, "There was so much going on—people here, things to look at there. I was quite overwhelmed. Quite." A bit sheepishly, he confessed, "I still don't really understand how Twitter works, but I suspect that someone else's feed looks very different from mine, and that even if I read the hashtag, there are still conversations and such I'm missing. Is that the way it works?"

At the end of the course, Graham said, the participants were asked to create an artifact to demonstrate their learning. Recalling that his daughter had recently created a music video for a school project of her own, Graham decided to put together a song composed of snippets of conversations he'd had during the course. "The music thing, that was a new direction. But I'd seen my daughter do it. I knew there was this thing—Alacrity, maybe it was called?—so I could just ask her about it." He did, and Graham's daughter installed the right software for him, which was actually named Audacity. "And even after she put it on my computer, a couple of times I just stood at the top of my study stairs and yelled 'Help!' So, I was lucky to have somebody like that to help me out. But being difficult didn't matter so much, because I wanted to do it."

Graham's second online learning experience was quite different. The course, "Understanding Dementia," was a much more typical one based on segmented topics, videos, and quizzes. "It made it easier to get what I wanted. I didn't have to jumble around to find information, it was all right there." But, frowning slightly, he also noted that "it just wasn't as much fun." Graham had enjoyed the conversations in the first class and thus had put a great deal of effort into talking with others in the forums in the second, responding to discussion threads, asking questions, and sharing his insights. He had found most co-participants very friendly. As for those who weren't, he wondered if perhaps there was something about the platform that made them unaware of their rudeness: "Perhaps they're just those chip-on-the-shoulder types who get by just fine in real life but who don't understand that you can't be like that online."

Used to reflecting on and analyzing his experiences, Graham ended the conversation by thinking aloud about the digital and learning skills and abilities needed by today's citizens. As he noted, this area "is an absolute ocean, and as you get more involved, you realize how much you've just dipped your toe in and there's so much more to learn. I sort of feel it's just responsible to have more understanding of your digital identity and to participate on the web." He saw this in part as a professional issue: "I just feel like I need to be on top of this so that I can teach my students how to be on top of this. It's digital literacy, whatever that means, the contemporary dimension of being literate. It's just the kind of literacy we need to have these days."

···

The digital literacy that Graham refers to has become a significant area of interest among researchers and something of a buzzword in education circles in recent years. Yet as Graham's words also reflect, many people remain confused as to just what digital literacy means. Although many authors have tried to disentangle its meanings (e.g., Bawden 2008), the term often remains elusive.

Literacy has traditionally been defined as the ability to read and write, a meaning that, over the past half century, has been expanded to include the ability to develop knowledge or competence in a particular area. Our understanding of literacy has thus widened to include terms like *visual literacy*, *technological literacy*, and *computer literacy*. The term *digital literacy* entered popular parlance through Gilster's 1997 book by the same name, where it is defined as "the ability to understand and use information in multiple formats from a wide range of sources when it is presented via computers" (1). Although, at the time, the internet still resembled the "one-to-one" or "one-to-many" pattern of traditional printed text, it has since evolved to enable "many-to-many" communication, thereby requiring skills, practices, habits, and understandings on the part of users that are much different from those of earlier forms of communication. And as digital technologies continue to evolve, what it means to be digitally literate has and will also continue to change.

One aspect of Glister's work that remains pertinent today is his distinction between two dimensions of digital literacy: skills and proficiencies with tools, which he called *mastering keystrokes,* and understanding and engaging with larger meanings of technology, which he termed *mastering ideas.* According to Belshaw (2014), these dimensions can be seen as two ends of a continuum ranging from literacy as a set of functional skills at one end to literacy as a social practice on the other.

The myriad definitions of digital literacy posited by researchers can be positioned along this continuum (e.g., Jenkins et al. 2006; Lankshear and Knobel 2013; Meyers, Erickson, and Small 2013; Stewart 2013; Bali 2016). A common element of these definitions, however, is that they generally understand digital literacies as *situated*—as differing by context and situation (Barton and Hamilton 2000; Beetham, McGill, and Littlejohn 2009; Meyers et al. 2013; Belshaw 2014).

To understand digital literacy in relation to online learning, therefore, we need to consider both its ethos and its technological components, which together constitute the skills, habits of mind, practices, and capabilities that allow learners to participate successfully in online courses.

Graham's story highlights a number of those components. To even enroll in an online course, regardless of whether it is a MOOC or a typical online course, learners need to draw upon a substantial set of digital skills: turning a computer on, using a mouse or touchpad, connecting to the internet, signing into a website, playing a video, responding to a comment, and so forth. That Graham didn't even mention these skills during the interview suggests he had become so proficient and comfortable with them that they had become automatic and taken for granted. Online courses, particularly less structured ones like the first one Graham took, often involve a variety of tools and applications that require participants to deploy a wide-ranging set of digital skills and proficiencies (Waite et al. 2013). Participants who don't have such skills, or the competence and confidence to develop them, can become overwhelmed or limit themselves to only a subset of the technologies and practices available in the course (Fini 2009). As Graham noted, he had to explore new technologies to participate in that class, and although he can tweet, he's still unsure about how Twitter actually "works."

Being able to interpret information is another key digital literacy required in online learning. Information literacy typically involves not only understanding or interpreting content but also identifying what information is needed, finding it, evaluating its reliability and appropriateness, and integrating it into the learner's existing knowledge. Graham's comparison of his experiences in his first class—where information was fragmented across a variety of spaces—with those in the second—where information was presented in a structured and sequenced manner—illustrates how some courses require higher levels of information literacy than others.

As Graham's story also illustrates, online learning increasingly requires a third set of literacies that we might term *literacies of participation*: the ability to create and present an online identity; to develop relationships with others from diverse backgrounds; and to share, collaborate, and contribute to a larger community or network. While some courses may be solitary and independent endeavors, researchers also note that online learning is a site of social engagement, interaction, and collaboration that requires that learners as well as instructors have the skills to facilitate such participation. That Graham encountered some participants who seemed to struggle with understanding the social conventions and cultural expectations of such online spaces demonstrates that those, too, are important components of this type of literacy. Literacies of participation also include the ability to connect with others and draw on the knowledge of networks to support learning, which is sometimes referred to as *relational agency* (Edwards 2005). Graham demonstrated this ability when he enlisted his daughter's knowledge and skill to help him create a song.

Digital literacies are neither novel nor unique to online courses but part of what are often termed "21st century learning skills" or "the capabilities which fit someone for living, learning and working in a digital society" (JISC 2015). Like many educators working in higher education, Graham is aware of the importance of helping students develop these skills. As he discovered, digital literacies are not only necessary but developed and enhanced through participating in online experiences. In his words, this is "just the kind of literacy we need to have these days."

...

- Digital literacies are essential for success in online learning contexts.
- While some learners may command such literacies, others may need support in developing them.

References

Bali, M. 2016. "Knowing the Difference between Digital Skills and Digital Literacies, and Teaching Both." *International Literacy Association*, February 3. http://literacyworldwide.org/blog /literacy-daily/2016/02/03/knowing-the-difference-between -digital-skills-and-digital-literacies-and-teaching-both.

Barton, D., and Hamilton, M. 2000. "Literacy Practices." In *Situated Literacies: Reading and Writing in Context*, edited by D. Barton, M. Hamilton, and R. Ivanic, 7–15. New York: Routledge.

Bawden, D. 2008. "Origins and Concepts of Digital Literacy." In *Digital Literacies: Concepts, Policies and Practices*, edited by C. Lankshear and M. Knobel, 17–32. New York: Peter Lang.

Beetham, H., McGill, L., and Littlejohn, A. H. 2009. *Thriving in the 21st Century: Learning Literacies for the Digital Age (LLiDA project)*. Glasgow: Glasgow Caledonian University.

Belshaw, D. 2014. *The Essential Elements of Digital Literacies*. Privately published e-book. www.dougbelshaw.com/ebooks.

Edwards, A. 2005. "Relational Agency: Learning to Be a Resourceful Practitioner." *International Journal of Educational Research* 43 (3): 168–182.

Fini, A. 2009. "The Technological Dimension of a Massive Open Online Course: The Case of the CCK08 Course Tools." *International Review of Research in Open and Distributed Learning* 10 (5).

Gilster, P. 1997. *Digital Literacy*. New York: John Wiley.

Jenkins, H., Clinton, K., Purushotma, R., Robinson, A. J., and Weigel, M. 2006. "Confronting the Challenges of Participatory Culture: Media Education for the 21st Century." *MacArthur Foundation*. http://www.digitallearning.macfound.org/.

JISC. 2015. "Developing Students' Digital Literacies." September 22. https://www.jisc.ac.uk/guides/developing-students-digital -literacy.

Lankshear, C., and Knobel, M. 2013. *A New Literacies Reader: Educational Perspectives*. New York: Peter Lang International Academic Publishers.

Meyers, E., Erickson, I., and Small, R. V. 2013. "Digital Literacy and Informal Learning Environments: An Introduction." *Learning, Media and Technology* 38 (4): 355–367. doi:10.1080/17439884.2013.783597

Stewart, B. 2013. "Massiveness + Openness = New Literacies of Participation?" *Journal of Online Learning and Teaching* 9 (2): 228–238.

Waite, M., Mackness, J., Roberts, G., and Lovegrove, E. 2013. "Liminal Participants and Skilled Orienteers: Learner Participation in a MOOC for New Lecturers." *Journal of Online Learning and Teaching* 9 (2): 200–215.

7.
The Learner Who Watched Videos Alone

In an article titled "The Early Days of Videotaped Lectures," Watters (2013) describes how, while completing her undergraduate degree via distance education in the 1990s, she took Introduction to Statistics, a prerequisite course for undergraduate students that, both then and now, is often taken in distance or online settings. I am including her story here because Watters discusses in a particularly evocative manner how lonely and solitary her online learning experience was. Loneliness crops up frequently in the distance and online education literature and is a topic that many researchers and practitioners have attempted to rectify.

For this course, Watters "was shipped a textbook, a package of worksheets, and a box of 20 some-odd videotapes. Watch the lectures. Take the quizzes. Mail them to the professor, who'd grade them and send them back." This design was, and in plenty cases still is, typical. Being able to "pause, rewind, and replay the videos" for this course was, she writes, "part of my rationale for signing up for this particular offering.

I'd heard that the instructor at the local community college wasn't that great, and while I had no idea if the professor from the university offering the correspondence course would be better, I trusted that the technology would make it easier for me to work through any confusion."

If she didn't understand the explanation the first time, or the second, she could "hit pause, rewind, and replay over and over and over. It's still the same lecture, still the same explanation."

What she hadn't expected, however, was the loneliness and crude repetitiveness of this approach:

> I watched the videos of "Introduction to Statistics" alone. (Paused, rewound, and replayed.) There was no way for me to stop the lecture to ask the professor a question. There were no office hours. There were no classmates with whom I could study.
>
> But there *was* the Internet. There *was* the Web.
>
> Yes, even decades ago there were bulletin boards and forums and chat rooms that (conceivably) I could have turned to for assistance. ("Help! I don't understand this question about standard deviation!")
>
> But I didn't. I watched the videos alone. I struggled. I paused, rewound, and replayed. I learned alone.
>
> Watching videos alone. Learning alone.

She compares this experience to a more recent one in a MOOC with thousands of students in which she "felt a very similar isolation, a similar distance from the professor and my peers as I did with that stack of videotapes and textbooks." Despite more than two decades of study and innovation in distance education, despite millions of dollars in funding that entrepreneurial endeavors, such as MOOCs, have received, lonely online learning experiences aren't long gone. To be certain, this is not a MOOC-specific problem. It is an online learning problem. While learning alone may work well for some groups of students, such solitary endeavors are a problem for most students: they limit their learning, discourage them from taking more online courses, and keep them from finishing.

...

Online learners face several challenges. These might include feelings of low confidence, a lack of adequate interaction with the instructor, lack of adequate support services (e.g., technical support), and so on. One area of significant concern that has been noted in the literature is student feelings of loneliness and isolation (Galusha 1997). As we will see in chapter 8, negative feelings, such as those of loneliness and isolation, are a problem because they impact cognition, satisfaction, persistence, and completion, adversely impacting students' learning experiences and outcomes.

Within online learning, Shin (2003) defined *isolation* or *loneliness* as "a subjective experience of lacking social support networks within which one can participate rather than meaning 'being alone'" (72). Croft, Dalton, and Grant (2010) note that feelings of isolation result from a complex interweaving of factors within the online environment. These factors include not only temporal and spatial dispersal, but also lack of social and sensory awareness of others, such as, for example, not being able to recognize whether peers are present and studying the same topic as you. Because of the diverse factors that may contribute to feelings of isolation, Shin (2003) and others suggest that, more than anything else, students need to feel connected to the institution, to peers, and to faculty. Shin saw student support through the institution as an important factor in developing a *transactional presence*—how connected a student feels online. Shin explained that if students have high feelings of transactional presence with their peers, they will be more satisfied, and such satisfaction may, in turn, lead to greater success at the course level and continued enrollment at the institutional level.

This poses the following conundrum for institutions: how do institutions meet students' needs for individual flexibility while developing and fostering a community that supports them in feeling connected at the same time? While some universities seek to maximize flexibility in order to satisfy students' individual needs—through design decisions that emphasize student autonomy, such as providing flexible course start dates, self-pacing, and dedicating the bulk of the coursework to be composed of individual work—other institutions sacrifice some flexibility in an attempt to reduce feelings of isolation (e.g., through synchronous courses or collaborative work). For example, many institutions, including Royal Roads University where I am currently employed, seek to develop learning communities in their online programs in an effort to alleviate feelings of isolation (Liu et al. 2007; Weiss 2000). As feelings of isolation can contribute to attrition (e.g., Ludwig-Hardman and Dunlap 2003) and as efforts to reduce isolation through collaborative and synchronous work may restrict the flexibility that online courses are purported to offer, institutions, instructors, and instructional designers need to strike a balance between their desire to offer flexible pathways to education and limit students' feelings of isolation.

To do so, online learning requires new kinds of pedagogies, ones that are reimagined for the digital age, meet the needs of students, capitalize on emerging technologies, and do not leave students feeling isolated (Anderson 2016; Bates 2015). As Morris and Stommel (2013) argue, "We must conceive of the activity of teaching, as an occupation and preoccupation, in entirely new and unexpected ways." Toward this goal, many researchers and educators have attempted to find ways to enhance interactions between instructors, students, and peers while also trying to encourage the development of communities and the cultivation of rich relationships within their online programs without sacrificing student agency and flexibility. The increasing consensus in the field is that high-quality online learning involves guided and fruitful back-and-forth interactions between learners, instructors, and peers. Pina (2019) highlights this point when he notes that "any discussion forum that instructs students to 'read all posts and respond to two'—without providing guidance as to what that response should be, can rightly be dismissed as mere busy-work." Long gone are the days where the primary purpose of distance education was to provide students with access to educational materials or a forum where they could post their reflections on the day's readings.

Learning designers and instructors have developed a number of ways for students to participate in rich interactions. One approach is to use discussion forums for activities that foster meaningful social interaction; for instance, by inviting students to share personal experiences related to a topic of study or to engage collaboratively in problem-solving. Another approach involves educators encouraging interactions between participants through the use of popular social and digital technologies, including podcasts, video-sharing platforms such as YouTube, and social networking sites such as Facebook and Twitter. According to the literature, when used in a pedagogical manner, such approaches can be effective in creating community and reducing feelings of anxiety and isolation (Kenney, Kumar, and Hart 2013; Kuyath, Mickelson, Saydam, and Winter 2013; Lee and Chan 2007). Moreover, such tools can extend students' interactions to include individuals outside the metaphorical walls of their institution, bridging what happens in the classroom or at their institution with events outside of it. For instance, doctoral students may experience feelings of isolation in their departments when they are the only ones studying a topic or are part of a small cohort, but some have employed Twitter to connect with others who are in similar situations (Ford, Veletsianos, and Resta 2014). Morris and Stommel (2013) go so far as to argue that "we need a larger discussion about the future of online education that privileges these [virtual] spaces as central and indispensable to learning" and that a "truly successful online program pays attention to what's already happening in digital culture," such as incorporating blogs and social media into online learning environments (see chapter 13). We *need* to pay attention to digital cultures because developments in that area not only reveal the realities that students will face outside of higher education institutions, but demonstrate how people may find community and build strong and thriving relationships online. Since the days of correspondence courses described by Watters, developments in social technologies and active pedagogies have changed the way we think about *distance* in distance education by making interactions between individuals much more immediate. But despite the seemingly evident benefits of leveraging social media in online education, Mnkandla and Minaar (2017) found that many online instructors lacked the technological and social media skills to effectively use social media as a pedagogical tool. Thus, they advised that instructors learn how to employ social media "to effectively facilitate social learning, collaboration, and interaction among students and between students and lecturers to enhance deep learning in a safe environment." In other words, to reduce student isolation and raise connectedness, instructors, and not just students, need the kind of digital literacies that Graham describes in chapter 6.

Another way to help combat isolation in the online space recommended by researchers is to build a learning community *within* an online course. Rovai (2002) has identified four dimensions of such a sense of community: classroom spirit, trust, interaction, and a commonality of expectations and goals. Without these, according to Rovai, students may feel more isolated, lonely, have lower self-esteem, and thus be unmotivated and potentially drop out of a course. Yet it is the quality and not merely the quantity of classroom interactions that contribute toward developing a community, requiring careful attention to course design and pedagogy. One strategy Rovai recommends to enhance a sense of community within online learning is organizing students into "a variety of learning activities such as student- or teacher-led discussion groups, debates, projects, and collaborative learning groups" in which the instructor can act as "encourager, harmonizer, compromiser, gatekeeper, standard setter, observer, or follower" to promote and maintain dialogue between students (9). Cormier (2008) believes that when participants negotiate knowledge and understanding, and produce content that is shared and interacted with collaboratively by their peers, the curriculum no longer merely consists of experts and content, but the community *becomes* the curriculum.

One final way to address loneliness and isolation that researchers recommend is for students to pursue several forms of emotional support through, for example, the formation of study groups. Holder (2007, 255) finds that "having the experience of a supportive group of friends and family and the comfort of knowing that they are not alone in this learning process was a significant function related to students' persistence." Seeking social and emotional support has also become an oft-repeated recommendation in MOOC settings, wherein some have recommended that learners enroll in MOOCs as part of a group or enlist their friends in their learning endeavors (e.g., Pickard 2016).

Online learning environments may be isolating and lonely, but emerging pedagogical approaches that support participation, community-building, and meaningful interactions can alleviate such feelings. As Watters reflected about her feelings of isolation while watching videos alone, "Part of this a failure of instructional design. Part of this is a failure of pedagogy. Part of it is a failure of community—a failure of both certain online education startups in fostering community and a failure on my part in joining it." Finding ways to address that failure while also meeting the desire for flexible learning that accommodates learners' needs is another of the challenges facing online education today.

...

- Student loneliness and isolation are negative feelings often associated with online learning contexts.
- Interventions aimed at increasing feelings of connectedness online learners feel with peers, faculty, and the institution may address feelings of learner isolation.
- Efforts at reducing transactional distance may encroach upon other valued aspects of online learning (e.g., flexibility).
- We need new pedagogical approaches, ones that are fit, and are developed for, the digital age, ones that emphasize connectedness.

References

Anderson, T. 2016. "Theories for Learning with Emerging Technologies." In *Emergence and Innovation in Digital Learning: Foundations and Applications*, edited by G. Veletsianos, 35–50. Alberta: Athabasca University Press.

Bates, T. 2015. *Teaching in a Digital Age: Guidelines for Designing Teaching and Learning for a Digital Age.* Victoria: BCcampus Open Textbooks.

Cormier, D. 2008. "Rhizomatic Education: Community as Curriculum." *Innovate: Journal of Online Education* 4 (5): 2. https://nsuworks.nova.edu/cgi/viewcontent.cgi?article=1045&context=innovate.

Croft, N., Dalton, A., and Grant, M. 2010. "Overcoming Isolation in Distance Learning: Building a Learning Community through Time and Space." *Journal for Education in the Built Environment* 5 (1): 27–64.

Ford, K. C., Veletsianos, G., and Resta, P. 2014. "The Structure and Characteristics of #PhDChat, an Emergent Online Social Network." *Journal of Interactive Media in Education* 2014 (1). http://doi.org/10.5334/2014-08.

Galusha, J. 1997. "Barriers to Learning in Distance Education." *Interpersonal Computing & Technology* 5 (3–4): 6–14.

Holder, B. 2007. "An Investigation of Hope, Academics, Environment, and Motivation as Predictors of Persistence in Higher Education Online Programs." *Internet and Higher Education* 10 (4): 245–260.

Kenney, J., Kumar, S., and Hart, M. 2013. "More Than a Social Network: Facebook as a Catalyst for an Online Educational Community of Practice." *International Journal of Social Media and Interactive Learning Environments* 1 (4): 355–369.

Kuyath, S. J., Mickelson, R. A., Saydam, C., and Winter, S. J. 2013. "The Effects of Instant Messaging on Distance Learning Outcomes." *International Journal of Business, Humanities and Technology* 3 (2): 13–26.

Lee, M. J., and Chan, A. 2007. "Reducing the Effects of Isolation and Promoting Inclusivity for Distance Learners through Podcasting." *Online Submission* 8 (1): 85–105.

Liu, X., Magjuka, R. J., Bonk, C. J., and Lee, S. 2007. "Does Sense of Community Matter? An Examination of Participants' Perceptions of Building Learning Communities in Online Courses." *Quarterly Review of Distance Education* 8 (1): 9–24.

Ludwig-Hardman, S., and Dunlap, J. 2003. "Learner Support Services for Online Students: Scaffolding for Success." *International Review of Research in Open and Distributed Learning* 4 (1). https://doi.org/10.19173/irrodl.v4i1.131.

Mnkandla, E., and Minaar, A. 2017. "The Use of Social Media in e-Learning: A Meta-synthesis." *International Review of Research in Open and Distributed Learning* 18 (5). http://www.irrodl.org/index.php/irrodl/article/view/3014/4293.

Morris, S. M., and Stommel, J. 2013. "Why Online Programs Fail and 5 Things We Can Do about It." *Hybrid Pedagogy* (blog), April 8. http://hybridpedagogy.org/why-online-programs-fail-and-5-things-we-can-do-about-it/.

Pickard, L. 2016. "MOOC Motivation Hacks: 30 Tips and Tricks to Keep You on Task." *ClassCentral*. https://www.classcentral.com/report/mooc-motivation-hacks/.

Pina, A. 2019, comment on Mark Lieberman, "Discussion Boards: Valuable? Overused? Discuss." *Inside Higher Education*, March 27. https://www.insidehighered.com/digital-learning/article/2019/03/27/new-approaches-discussion-boards-aim-dynamic-online-learning#comment-4399067465.

Rovai, A. 2002. "Building Sense of Community at a Distance." *International Review of Research in Open and Distance Learning* 3 (1): 1–16.

Shin, N. 2003. "Transactional Presence as a Critical Predictor of Success in Distance Learning." *Distance Education* 24 (1): 69–86.

Watters, A. 2013. "The Early Days of Videotaped Lectures." *Hybrid Pedagogy* (blog), April 11. https://hybridpedagogy.org/the-early-days-of-videotaped-lectures/.

Weiss, R. E. 2000. "Humanizing the Online Classroom." In *Principles of Effective Teaching in the Online Classroom*, edited by R. E. Weiss, D. S. Knowlton, and B. W. Speck, 47–51. San Francisco: Jossey-Bass.

8.

The Learner Who Showed Emotion

Many individuals view online learning as transactional, as encompassing a transaction between two parties—student and instructor, student and institution—in a similar way that banking encompasses a transaction between two parties—bank and client, accountholder and accountholder. The proliferation of websites selling information products masquerading as "courses" reinforces this belief. This perspective often overlooks the difficulties with even these kinds of seemingly simple, practical transactions. Have you ever tried to send money to someone abroad or to open an account in a country to which you just arrived? This perspective—online learning as transactional—does not seem to align with what I have observed and experienced in online learning environments.

A few years ago, I sat in a row, next to two colleagues, facing a large monitor and a webcam. The three of us, who made up the examining committee for Magda's thesis, had just finished our deliberations following an hour-long examination. Magda was one of my supervisees, an online student I'd interacted with via phone, audio-conference, and email many times but never seen until that day. At this point, she was sitting at home waiting for us to invite her to log back online so we could give her the results of our deliberations.

When my colleague placed the call, Magda quickly appeared on the video screen and, her voice trembling, announced, "I'm back."

As the supervisor, it was my responsibility to deliver the news: "We have discussed your thesis and presentation. I'm excited to tell you that we are recommending only minor revisions for your thesis, and as such, you'll be able to quickly wrap this up. Congratulations, Magda! You should be proud of this work."

She stared at me for what seemed like a long time but, in reality, was but a second or two. Then, tears filling her eyes, she responded, "We did it, George, we did it!" I smiled at her and replied, "*You* did it, Magda. I just supported you along the way." As her tears continued to flow, now accompanied by a warm smile, she chuckled and informed us that her partner was silently cheering her from behind the screen. My colleagues then congratulated her as well, and I promised to follow up our conversation that afternoon with a detailed email as to what revisions were required to the thesis before hanging up.

When I turned to one of my colleagues, I saw her eyes had also grown misty. "It's been a long journey," I said, my voice breaking as I added, "Magda had to take quite some time off for a variety of personal concerns. But here she is, stronger than ever." My own eyes teared up as I thought about the challenges that Magda had overcome and the magnitude of her achievement despite the adversities she faced. Although many people assume that online learning is a dry and detached process, a transaction to obtain a credential, this view overlooks the role of emotion in the ongoing process of learning regardless of whether it takes place online or not.

...

As Magda's story points out, online learning, like all learning, can be what Sharpe and Benfield (2005) have described as an emotionally charged experience. Learners' emotions related to their online studies can vary from frustration, to joy, to anxiety, to a sense of warmth and belongingness. Online learning is not the detached, unemotional, and dry experience it is often imagined to be. Recognizing that online learning is emotionally charged is to acknowledge the humanity of it, and this is important because it may enable us to strengthen our relationships with our students, and, in the process, improve the quality of our emotional relationships and our educational programming.

Historically, emotion and cognition have been considered separate domains and emotion often viewed as something that impairs cognition, rational thought, and learning (Cleveland-Innes and Campbell 2012). In an article in the *New York Times* entitled "Students Learn from People They Love," David Brooks writes, "Teaching consisted of dispassionately downloading knowledge into students' brains. Then work by cognitive scientists like Antonio Damasio showed us that emotion is not the opposite of reason; it's essential to reason. Emotions assign value to things." In fact, many scholars have begun to acknowledge and examine the more complex role that emotion actually plays in learning (e.g., MacFadden 2005, 2007), demonstrating the "centrality of emotion in many cognitive processes" (O'Regan 2003, 80). Emotion not only shapes individuals' cognition but the social interactions necessary for building conceptual understanding (Delahunty,

Verenikina, and Jones 2014). Indeed, research has shown that emotion impacts such diverse aspects of learning as motivation (Dirkx 2006), choice of learning experiences (Artino 2010), self-regulation (Pekrun et al. 2010), and social interaction (Cleveland-Innes and Campbell 2012).

Despite the increasing recognition of the importance of emotion in learning, the learning that takes place in online spaces is most often depicted in the literature as less emotionally rich, more impersonal, and less influenced by emotion than learning that takes place in-person. This view is reflected, for instance, in work that describes face-to-face teaching as innately human, in contrast to the "online medium [which] will make us miss, misread or simply not recognize" human feelings (Mentz and Schaberg 2018). The implication here is that the medium is not simply impersonal but actually lacks, masks, and hides emotions. Similar to schooling which Valenzuela (2010) sees as organized in ways that deprives youth of their cultures, languages, and identities, online learning is often perceived to be subtractive in a different way—as abating learners and instructors of the human interaction involved in teaching and learning. But as Delahunty, Verenikina, and Jones (2014) argue, all learning is a personal and social experience that involves physical, cognitive, social, and emotional factors. In online spaces, the socio-emotional aspects of learning become even more, not less, important for instructors and learners.

This recognition has led a number of scholars to turn their attention to the kinds of emotions that learners experience in online learning. In an early study on this topic, O'Regan (2003) uncovered that online learners experienced a range of emotions during their learning experiences, from frustration (the most common emotion, reported by all the students) and anxiety to enthusiasm and pride. Many of the negative emotions chronicled by O'Regan—and later scholars such as Artino and Jones (2012) and MacFadden (2005, 2007)—were related to the technology used: problems with reliability, lack of familiarity, system glitches, needing to trust unknown systems, and reliance on text-based media. A study by Zembylas (2008) also found that adult online learners experienced emotions such as anxiety, stress, and guilt in relation to their difficulties in balancing their various life roles and responsibilities, as well as to technology use. Importantly, however, Zembylas also found that learners' negative emotions gradually decreased over the duration of the course as the students became more familiar with online communication and that they increasingly expressed positive emotions such as joy, pride, and satisfaction about the flexibility of online learning, completing course requirements, and the support they gained from their relationships with other learners.

Much of the literature in this area draws upon the control-value model of emotion (Pekrun 2006), which suggests that a learner's emotions are influenced by their evaluation of the control they have over their learning and the value they place on the experience. Research by Artino and Jones (2012) describes a complex relationship between emotions and achievement in which emotions that are generally considered negative (e.g., boredom, frustration) led to the use of self-regulated learning strategies and higher achievement, resulting in learners experiencing positive emotions like pride and confidence. Similarly, research by You (2012) and You and Kang (2014) found that positive and negative emotions mediated the relationship between a learner's perceptions of academic control and their use of self-regulated learning strategies. The relationship between positive emotion and perceived control is not restricted to the academic component of online learning: Butz, Stupnisky, and Pekrun (2015) noted that learners who saw themselves as confident with technology were more likely to have positive emotions and feel successful in their online learning experiences.

Researchers have also examined how emotion is related to the learning community of a course and the social aspects of online learning. The findings of Delahunty et al. (2014) suggest that interaction with others is an essential part of learning, as they show that online learners often describe feelings of disconnection and isolation as major impediments to their online learning. Scholarship on the socio-emotional aspects of online learning has frequently used a community of inquiry framework to investigate how the notion of presence is developed in online learning settings (Garrison, Anderson, and Archer 1999). Angelaki and Mavroidis (2013), for instance, found that social connections and communication with peers played an important role in the emotional well-being of online learners. Such findings seem to affirm the suggestion made by Cleveland-Innes and Campbell (2012) that emotion underpins the entire experience of learning online and that emotional presence should thus be considered a foundational component of online learning.

In addition to studies that have explored the role of emotion in formal online learning, a few have extended that investigation to other digital learning settings, such as MOOCs. For example, drawing on the popular control-value framework, Dillon et al. (2016) asked learners in a statistics MOOC to identify their emotions in relation to both specific aspects of the course and the course overall. These authors found that positive emotions (e.g., hope, enjoyment, contentment) were common, while negative emotions (e.g., disappointment, anger, shame) were rare. This finding is somewhat contradictory of earlier studies that have uncovered negative emotions related to feelings of isolation or alienation in MOOCs and online learning more generally (Zutshi et al. 2013; Delahunty et al. 2014; Mackness and Bell 2015). Findings in the MOOC literature are generally mixed: While much of the literature seems to indicate that participants are more likely to report experiencing positive than negative emotions (e.g., Zutshi, O'Hare, and Rodafinos 2013; Koutropoulos et al. 2014), many researchers show that learners report negative emotions resulting from challenges they face such as lack of structure (Liu et al. 2015) and technological difficulties (Fini 2009).

Mackness and Bell (2015) describe the broader literature succinctly when they find that different participants often had very different emotional experiences. Like Zembylas (2008), however, Dillon and colleagues (2016) found that the emotions reported by participants fluctuated over the duration of the course and in relation to differing aspects of the course, and that negative emotions were significantly correlated with dropping out of the course. In an ethnographic study analyzing forum posts, Cheng (2014) found that more than half of the forum posts analyzed contained some expression of emotion (e.g., a description of feelings, suggestion of a specific emotional state, or use of an emoticon), and that most emotions were positive. What these studies reveal is that emotions can't be separated from online learning. Whether a learner experiences altruism, connectedness, acceptance by others, hope, despair, or other less intense emotions, recognizing emotions as an integral part of learning should compel us to approach the design of learning experiences, the act of online teaching, and the creation of online programs with a sense of humility and care for learners.

Recognizing and acknowledging that online learning is an emotionally charged experience for learners has significant implications for instructors, designers, researchers, and the field writ large. Above all, this recognition casts doubt on the view that online learning is merely transactional. Online learning is often dubbed a "delivery mechanism," a way to deliver education to students in the same way that a mailperson delivers mail to one's residence. The literature reviewed above shows that online learning, to students, isn't merely transactional: it facilitates excitement, passion, frustration, and a whole slew of emotions.

...

- Online learning is an emotionally charged experience and is often much more than a transaction.
- Since emotions are an integral part of learning, we should approach the design of online learning with care and humility.

References
Angelaki, C., and Mavroidis, I. 2013. "Communication and Social Presence: The Impact on Adult Learners' Emotions in Distance Learning." *European Journal of Open, Distance and E-learning* 16 (1): 78–93.

Artino, A. R. 2010. "Online or Face-to-Face Learning? Exploring the Personal Factors That Predict Students' Choice of Instructional Format." *Internet and Higher Education* 13 (4): 272–276. http://doi.org/10.1016/j.iheduc.2010.07.005.

Artino, A. R., and Jones, K. D. 2012. "Exploring the Complex Relations between Achievement Emotions and Self-Regulated Learning Behaviors in Online Learning." *Internet and Higher Education* 15 (3): 170–175. http://doi.org/10.1016/j.iheduc.2012.01.006.

Butz, N. T., Stupnisky, R. H., and Pekrun, R. 2015. "Students' Emotions for Achievement and Technology Use in Synchronous Hybrid Graduate Programmes: A Control-Value Approach." *Research in Learning Technology* 23.

Cheng, J. C. 2014. "An Exploratory Study of Emotional Affordance of a Massive Open Online Course." *European Journal of Open, Distance and e-Learning*, 17 (1): 43–55.

Cleveland-Innes, M., and Campbell, P. 2012. "Emotional Presence, Learning, and the Online Learning Environment." *International Review of Research in Open and Distributed Learning* 13 (4): 269–292.

Delahunty, J., Verenikina, I., and Jones, P. 2014. "Socio-emotional Connections: Identity, Belonging and Learning in Online Interactions—a Literature Review." *Technology, Pedagogy and Education* 23 (2): 243–265.

Dillon, J., Bosch, N., Chetlur, M., Wanigasekara, N., Ambrose, G. A., Sengupta, B., and D'Mello, S. K. 2016. "Student Emotion, Co-occurrence, and Dropout in a MOOC Context." *International Educational Data Mining Society*. https://files.eric.ed.gov/fulltext/ED592723.pdf.

Dirkx, J. M. 2006. "Engaging Emotions in Adult Learning: A Jungian Perspective on Emotion and Transformative Learning." *New Directions for Adult and Continuing Education* 109: 15–26.

Fini, A. 2009. "The Technological Dimension of a Massive Open Online Course: The Case of the CCK08 Course Tools." *International Review of Research in Open and Distributed Learning* 10 (5).

Garrison, D. R., Anderson, T., and Archer, W. 1999. "Critical Inquiry in a Text-Based Environment: Computer Conferencing in Higher Education." *Internet and Higher Education* 2 (2–3): 87–105.

Koutropoulos, A., Abajian, S. C., Hogue, R. J., Keskin, N. O., and Rodriguez, C. O. 2014. "What Tweets Tell Us about MOOC Participation." *International Journal of Emerging Technologies in Learning (iJET)* 9 (1): 8–21.

Liu, M., Kang, J., and McKelroy, E. 2015. "Examining Learners' Perspective of Taking a MOOC: Reasons, Excitement, and Perception of Usefulness." *Educational Media International* 52 (2): 129–146.

MacFadden, R. J. 2005. "Souls on Ice: Incorporating Emotion in Web-Based Education." *Journal of Technology in Human Services* 23 (1–2): 79–98. http://doi.org/10.1300/J017v23n01_06.

MacFadden, R. J. 2007. "The Forgotten Dimension in Learning: Incorporating Emotion into Web-Based Education." *Journal of Technology in Human Services* 25 (1–2): 85–101.

Mackness, J., and Bell, F. 2015. "Rhizo14: A Rhizomatic Learning cMOOC in Sunlight and in Shade." *Open Praxis* 7 (1): 25–38.

Mentz, S., and Schaberg, C. 2018. "Online Learning: A 2-Voiced Case for Ambivalence." *Inside Higher Education* (blog), December 4. https://www.insidehighered.com/views/2018/12/04/two-scholars -debate-pros-and-cons-online-learning-opinion.

O'Regan, K. 2003. "Emotion and e-Learning." *Journal of Asynchronous Learning Network* 59 (3): 513–528. http://doi.org/10.1037 /a0020172.

Pekrun, R. 2006. "The Control-Value Theory of Achievement Emotions: Assumptions, Corollaries, and Implications for Educational Research and Practice." *Educational Psychology Review* 18 (4): 315–341.

Pekrun, R., Goetz, T., Daniels, L. M., Stupnisky, R. H., and Perry, R. P. 2010. "Boredom in Achievement Settings: Exploring Control-Value Antecedents and Performance Outcomes of a Neglected Emotion." *Journal of Educational Psychology* 102 (3): 531–549.

Sharpe, R., and Benfield, G. 2005. "The Student Experience of e-Learning in Higher Education." *Brookes eJournal of Learning and Teaching* 1 (3). http://bejlt.brookes.ac.uk/paper/reflections-on-the -student-experience-of-e-learning-in-higher-education-a-review -of-the-literature/.

You, J. W., and Kang, M. 2014. "The Role of Academic Emotions in the Relationship between Perceived Academic Control and Self-Regulated Learning in Online Learning." *Computers and Education*, 77: 125–133. http://doi.org/10.1016/j.compedu.2014.04 .018.

Valenzuela, A. 2010. *Subtractive Schooling: US-Mexican Youth and the Politics of Caring*. Albany: State University of New York Press.

You, J. 2012. "The Structural Relationship among Task Value, Self-Efficacy, Goal Structure, and Academic Emotions for Promoting Self-Regulated Learning in e-Learning Course." *The Journal of Korean Association of Computer Education* 16 (4): 61–77.

Zembylas, M. 2008. "Adult Learners' Emotions in Online Learning." *Distance Education* 29 (1): 71–87. http://doi.org/10.1080 /01587910802004852.

Zutshi, S., O'Hare, S., and Rodafinos, A. 2013. "Experiences in MOOCs: The Perspective of Students." *American Journal of Distance Education* 27 (4): 218–227.

9.
The Learner Who "Listened"

Though we had agreed to use Skype for our interview, Angie had requested that we not use video during our conversation. I was happy to extend that accommodation, and her reasons for this request became clear during our interview. Those reasons illustrate that there are valuable ways to learn beyond class participation and that accommodate learners' needs.

Living in the United Kingdom and in her early forties, Angie was reticent to share much about her employment or other background, noting that her work related to law enforcement and that she wasn't able to tell me much more about it. Sensing her desire to hold back on personal details, I quickly transitioned our conversation into the online course she was currently taking. These three general bits of self-reported information (age, location, and employment at the time) are all that I know about Angie as far as demographics are concerned.

The course that Angie was enrolled in included collaborative activities and opportunities to interact with instructional staff, such as a vibrant discussion board. Angie elected not to participate and, in fact, was pleased that interaction with others was an optional aspect of the course. This became clear when I asked her to describe to me any difficulties she faced in the course. "I wouldn't call them difficulties," she said reluctantly, "Basically, I'm very introverted, and for me, it's difficult communicating with other people. So, I'm not able to discuss different things, like on forums with other people, because I'm losing focus. I prefer to learn on my own without discussing anything. It's something that I'd like to work on."

In wanting to learn more about her participation in the course, I asked what she would do if she did not understand materials that were assigned in the course. She paused. Eventually she said, "If I don't understand, I just . . . Nothing I can do about it. I usually, I just continue to do the work, and . . . I try to understand only what I'm able to understand." Sometimes in interviews it helps to provide examples to people to clarify a question. I, therefore, told Angie that other people I have interviewed talk to family members and ask questions or ask questions on the discussion board. "Do you do any of those things," I inquired, "or perhaps something different?"

"Very rarely," she said, "because of my introversion. When there are videos, I watch them twice, and I read the discussion forums. But when I talk to people, I get distracted." She paused again. "And it's a big challenge for me, even talking to you. For me, it requires a lot of effort." It was my turn to pause. After a second or two, I expressed my appreciation for her time and effort, and for taking on what must have been an obstacle to have this conversation with me. She was very gracious in explaining that interactions with others don't come easy for her, but that she was grateful to participate in a learning experience that did not require her to interact with others in significant ways. As far as her performance in the course?

She was on track to complete it successfully and found that it had immediate practical relevance to her personal and professional life.

By examining the course log data, I confirmed that Angie never contributed content to the course site: she neither posted on the discussion board, nor added comments on other parts of the course. For all practical purposes, it seemed as if Angie was a fly on the wall, reading materials, watching tutorials and videos, engaging individually with the course content without being seen or heard by anyone other than the course instructor. She was listening, creating, and learning in a non-public way.

...

As discussed in prior chapters, researchers generally agree that interactions among students and between students and instructors are integral to the quality of online learning, and emerging forms of online pedagogy have, therefore, emphasized and encouraged learner participation and active engagement. To that end, online courses often require students to demonstrate their participation in visible ways, typically through contributions to discussion posts and so on. Lack of participation is widely considered a problem and is often described with the pejorative term *lurking*. Lack of participation may be an indicator that learners are facing challenges that prevent them from participating fully, are disengaged, are having troubles with the content of the course, or are otherwise falling behind. And the longer the inactivity lasts, the more challenging it may be for learners to catch up. In short, students who engage with the material are more likely to succeed. Full participation, Selwyn (2010) argues, is necessary for learning, imperative even, and especially so for certain populations such as younger students. Other researchers highlight further problems with lurking: Rovai (2000) considers lurking to negatively impact community-building and White (2015) argues that such behavior is often associated with "voyeurism and surveillance." Understandably, instructors, administrators, and researchers may be concerned when lurking reflects social loafing. Social loafing is the situation in which some people exert less effort to achieve a goal when they are in social situations, such as social and collaborative learning environments, than when they are alone. This is a problem because it may place a burden on some students to participate, may lead to lower achievement for groups of people working together, and may limit diversity of thought.

For all these reasons, the literature is replete with recommendations to discourage the type of behavior referred to as lurking and encourage active participation in online courses, all tackling a variety of perceived problems surrounding lack of participation, ranging from suggestions to create more engaging activities, develop a warm course community, explicitly state expectations, and incentivize participation through assigning grades to discussion board posts. The quintessential online learning activity that invites students to write a response to a prompt posted by the instructor followed by two replies to peers' responses reflects this exact idea, underpinned by the assumption that participation is worthwhile, interaction with others is valuable, and that participation and interaction can be encouraged through a structured approach to learning design.

The behavior that is often referred to as *lurking*, however, is not necessarily always a problem. For one, the term is pejorative. Instead of using the term lurking, some researchers have proposed alternative terms: Crawford (2009) suggests "listening" and Nonnecke and Preece (2003) recommend "non-public participation." Angie wasn't engaging in voyeurism and surveillance. She was listening and participating in ways that weren't publicly visible, in ways that made her feel comfortable. As several researchers have pointed out, to understand whether participating in this way is problematic, and to explore whether there may in fact be benefits for learners engaging in "silent" participation, it is important to understand the reasons why students choose to engage in these ways (e.g., Dennen 2008; Honeychurch, Bozkurt, Singh, and Koutropoulous 2017). In particular, the broader literature on lurking, shows that individuals lurk for a wide range of reasons (e.g., environmental and personal factors) and that, unlike broader assumptions that underpin beliefs about lack of participation, most lurkers are *not* selfishly taking advantage of discussions without contributing (Preece, Nonnecke, and Andrews 2004; Sun, Rau, and Ma 2014).

Engaging in "listening" or other nonpublic participatory behaviors online may not necessarily indicate lack of engagement or learning. After all, social learning theorists have long posited that a significant way in which people learn is through modeling the behavior of others, through observing and imitating others (Bandura 1971). In an examination of the various invisible ways in which some learners engage in online courses, and drawing on Lave and Wenger's (1991) notion of *communities of practice*, Honeychurch, Bozkurt, Singh, and Koutropoulos (2017) conceptualized lurkers as learners perched on the periphery of a community. These individuals learn online even when platforms and instructors are not able to identify or see their activities (Veletsianos, Collier, and Schneider 2015). For instance, some students in the aforementioned study described collaborating with other students outside the class platform on social media and in face-to-face spaces. White (2015) argues that these learners are not simply freeloading or loafing but critically evaluating the discourse in their field and waiting until they feel more confident before actively contributing, thereby moving from "knowledge-consumer to active community member" and reaching "the point at which they are exploring their 'voice' within the discourse." According to this view, these "silent" learners are simply attempting to understand, through observation and modeling from other participants, how the online community engages with one another. White thus reminds us that some learners prefer slow, purposeful, and timely participation rather than immediate participation, and thus the lack of public participation shouldn't automatically be considered a problem and perhaps it ought not to be discouraged. To this end, White coins the term *elegant lurking* to reflect a sort of graceful engagement with content that shuns the disturbing vibe that the term lurking seems to entail.

Even though the literature on online learning emphasizes active and visible participation, it is imperative to balance this emphasis with a recognition that there are other, and perhaps just as valuable and vital, ways to learn. Doing so recognizes the diversity of our students, enables us to be more inclusive, and perhaps even offers us an opportunity to explore pedagogical approaches that aren't focused on participation and public forms of interaction. As Dennen (2008, 1626) has pointed out, "The online class lurker has a corollary in classroom-based instruction, namely the student who sits silently throughout class session—and may even look bored—but who performs well on assessments." She found that students who took more time to read through other students' messages before posting themselves tended to find the discussion activity more worthwhile than students who read less before posting. This finding supports the conclusion that posting behavior alone may not always accurately reflect students' level of interest and engagement.

These scholars' work suggests that online course designers and instructors need to consider that visible public participation is only one form of engagement. Coupled with the recognition that learners intentionally and unintentionally engage in many activities that are invisible to both instructors and digital learning platforms, the solution isn't to attempt to make visible every interaction with content and every activity that occurs in the course of learning. Rather, we should approach learning with the diversity it deserves and consider how learners who are reticent to participate in public fora—or learners who, for whatever reason are *listening* rather than *talking*—are supported in their learning endeavors. One way to do so may be to provide choices for learners to decide how, when, and to what extent they'd like to engage with others. I explore this topic further in chapter 16.

...

- Lurking is widely perceived as problematic as it may be both an indicator of challenges learners face (e.g., disengagement) and may lead to additional problems (e.g., undue burden on others to contribute).
- Lurking, however, may not be an accurate description of one's behavior. For instance, learners may be "listening" or participating in ways that are not visible to the digital platform or to the instructor. Framed in this way, nonpublic participation may be a valid learning approach.
- The online learning literature emphasizes participation and interaction, but it may be worthwhile to consider that there are other, perhaps just as valuable and vital, ways to learn.

References

Bandura, A. 1971. *Psychological Modelling: Conflicting Theories.* Chicago: Aldine-Atherton.

Crawford, K. 2009. "Following You: Disciplines of Listening in Social Media." *Continuum* 23 (4): 525–535.

Dennen, V. P. 2008. "Pedagogical Lurking: Student Engagement in Non-posting Discussion Behavior." *Computers in Human Behavior* 24 (4): 1624–1633.

Honeychurch, S., Bozkurt, A., Singh, L., and Koutropoulos, A. 2017. "Learners on the Periphery: Lurkers as Invisible Learners." *European Journal of Open, Distance and e-Learning* 20 (1): 192–212. https://www.degruyter.com/downloadpdf/j/eurodl.2017.20.issue -1/eurodl-2017-0012/eurodl-2017-0012.pdf.

Lave, J., and Wenger, E. 1991. *Situated Learning: Legitimate Peripheral Participation.* Cambridge, UK: Cambridge University Press.

Nonnecke, B., and Preece, J. 2003. "Silent Participants: Getting to Know Lurkers Better." In *From Usenet to CoWebs: Interacting with Social Information Spaces*, edited by C. Leug and D. Fisher, 110–132. London: Springer.

Preece, J., Nonnecke, B., and Andrews, D. 2004. "The Top Five Reasons for Lurking: Improving Community Experiences for Everyone." *Computers in Human Behavior* 20 (2): 201–223.

Rovai, A. 2000. "Building and Sustaining Community in Asynchronous Learning Networks." *Internet and Higher Education* 3: 285–297.

Selwyn, N. 2010. "The Educational Significance of Social Media: A Critical Perspective." Keynote debate at Ed-Media Conference 2010, Toronto, Canada, June 28, 2019. http://www.scribd.com/doc /33693537/The-educational-significance-of-social-media-a-critical -perspective.

Sun, N., Rau, P. P. L., and Ma, L. 2014. "Understanding Lurkers in Online Communities: A Literature Review." *Computers in Human Behavior* 38: 110–117.

White, D. 2015. "Elegant Lurking." *Digital Learning Culture* (blog), April 16. http://daveowhite.com/elegant-lurking/.

Veletsianos, G., Collier, A., and Schneider, E. 2015. "Digging Deeper into Learners' Experience in MOOCs: Participation in Social Networks Outside of MOOCs, Notetaking, and Contexts Surrounding Content Consumption." *British Journal of Educational Technology* 46 (3): 570–587.

10.

The Learner Who Cheated

What follows is a disturbing and bizarre story told to me by an acquaintance who gave me his consent to include it here. Even though I can't verify the truthfulness of it, and can't be certain of the degree to which it is exaggerated or not, I have heard this story multiple times and the details of it are always consistent. Assuming that the story is truthful, my own impression is that this is a rare story. Regardless of its rarity, it is inexcusable. Nonetheless, I am sharing it here because it revealed to me possible ways in which a student in a face-to-face program which includes online components might cheat in a way that I had never dreamed of before. Unlike the rest of the stories in this book that focus on online students, this story centers around a student in face-to-face programs that included online components. I chose to include it because it highlights issues around academic dishonesty, as well as issues around the blurring of lines between in-person and online education.

...

A few years ago, on a warm spring day, I was having coffee with an acquaintance. James was having financial troubles, and I recommended he return to his private tutoring days, a practice that I knew had generated sufficient income for him in the past. "Working with one student would be helpful," he quipped. "What I need is a student that needs a lot of help, a student like Adrian." James then told me he had tutored Adrian through finance-related undergraduate and graduate degrees at two prestigious universities abroad. More specifically, James shared that he started off trying to tutor Adrian and maybe even started doing assignments for her as helpful examples. Eventually, he ended up doing the assignments. He sounded apologetic and frustrated. I was bewildered.

Adrian was interested in finance and in many ways was studious: she never missed class, studied day in and day out, and spent countless hours at the library. According to James, however, who incidentally is not an expert on these matters, Adrian had a learning disability and that meant she could never fully comprehend the language and topic of instruction. Regardless, a degree seemed like a necessity for someone who, upon graduation, was going to take on a job at the family's successful business.

Adrian's troubles should have been diagnosed by her institutions and instructors early on, perhaps as early as orientation week, but they seemingly never were. Instead, James helped her complete years of university courses without her truly engaging in critical or original examination of finance herself. James described in some detail the strategies they employed to avoid detection. Though her degree was face-to-face, all her courses included online components. Some of those courses included discussion forums on which he never once posted on her behalf, even though he emailed her replies to post on those forums. He would read lecture notes and use her digital credentials to access library resources. He would request books to be delivered to her, ask her to scan and email him parts of those books, write essays for her, and even conduct checks on his own work by submitting essays to plagiarism detection software prior to submission for grading. There were even times when he would help her compose emails. This operation—unethical as it was—was extensive, and according to James, the security checks conducted by her instructors were ineffective: Since James was completing every assignment, there was no inconsistency in the work. Though fraudulent, the work was consistent.

"So, you need another student that needs your help in cheating?" I asked in astonishment.

"No," James said emphatically, "I need students who need long-term tutoring—not just for an hour here and there—to make enough money. The cheating? It's depressing." It became clear to me that James had ethical qualms about this.

...

Academic dishonesty—including intentional and unintentional plagiarism, cheating, and unacknowledged collusion—is a growing concern among faculty and administrators, both in online and face-to-face contexts, as it appears that more and more students are engaging in such behavior. In a systematic analysis of data on student cheating since 1978, Newton (2018) found truth to the claim that cheating is on the rise. As Fusch, Ness, Booker, and Fusch (2017) point out, academic dishonesty is an "act of deception that inflicts moral harm on all parties by damaging the reputation of self and others, insulting others' intelligence, and harming the integrity of all" (55). As "operation varsity blues"—the 2019 college admissions bribery scandal in the United States—unambiguously revealed, the harms of dishonesty impact us all extensively: students, parents, institutional actors, and society more broadly. It's a societal problem for instance, for learners who cheat may not have the actual skills represented by their credentials. To address threats to academic integrity, it is important to understand the ways in which students are participating in these dishonest practices, why they choose to cheat, and what institutions can do to deter such behavior.

Many faculty members, administrators, students, business-people, and members of the public have the perception that cheating happens more in online courses than in face-to-face settings, based largely on the assumption that students who study alone without the checks and balances provided by an instructor may be more prone to cheating. The research evidence on this point is mixed and inconclusive but does show that academic dishonesty occurs in both online and face-to-face spaces (Black, Greaser, and Dawson 2008; Watson and Sottile 2010). Some studies have found that cheating is more prevalent in online courses (e.g., Lanier 2006), while others discovered that students in face-to-face courses cheated more than those in online courses (e.g., Peled, Eshet, Barczyk, and Grinautski 2019), and yet others found no significant differences in cheating between students enrolled in online and face-to-face programs (Ison 2014). As Adrian's story reveals, cheating may take place digitally even if a student is in a face-to-face context. As all courses nowadays are online to some degree (from students' use of digital technologies to retrieve resources to instructors' use of it to support teaching), it is increasingly difficult to draw demarcating lines between online and face-to-face courses and develop ways to combat cheating that solely happens in one context. The significant question becomes not whether students engage in more misconduct in one course mode than another but why they engage in misconduct at all and what we can do about it.

Some argue that students cheat in response to systemic problems facing higher education. In 2010, the *Chronicle of Higher Education* published an essay titled "The Shadow Scholar" in which a pseudonymous writer (who, a few years later, identified himself as Dave Tomar [Barrett 2012; McGee 2013]) detailed his practice of writing student papers through a custom-essay company (Dante 2010). For almost a decade, Tomar admitted in his essay, he had written hundreds of academic papers, including theses and dissertations, for students in business and nursing courses as well as for school principals and seminary students. He also reported completing online courses for clients using their login credentials. Tomar, citing his disillusionment with the institution of postsecondary education to justify his activities, claimed that cheating was "utterly consistent with everything else about college," with universities' focus on economic growth at the expense of the student, on grading above learning, and on institutional prestige above providing assistance and support to students who needed it most. Tomar, in other words, saw cheating as evidence of the system's own failures. For instance, he blamed universities for not adequately supporting the English-as-a-second-language students who hired him, arguing that universities had left it up to these students to master the language immediately or suffer the consequences. Thus, he placed the blame for such cheating not on himself or the students who sought his services, but on the institutions' focus on summative evaluation over authentic education. His rationale is consistent with the language that many contract cheating companies use to sell their services, which, Wendy-Sutherland (as cited in Schaffhauser 2018, para. 2) describes as follows, "We know the university hasn't got time to really help you. We know that you're struggling with timelines. We're here to help you with writing. We're available 24/7, which your university professors are not."

The research literature, however, identifies many factors that are linked to the practice of cheating, only some of which are institutional. These factors include pressures to succeed; the nature of certain assessment practices that require information regurgitation and inauthentic application of knowledge; individual students' morals, cultural background, and time constraints; a lack of significant consequences for dishonesty; and students' lack of understanding of what actually constitutes cheating behavior. In a study of cheating among business students, for instance, Simkin and McLeod (2010) found that academic dishonesty was driven by students' desire to succeed: "if 'winning is everything,' then cheating simply becomes a tool to use in pursuit of this higher goal" (443). Batane (2010), in contrast, found that students used cheating primarily as a way to save time; as one student stated, "We have many other assignments that we have to do, so getting material from the internet saves you a lot of time to do other things" (7). McGee (2013) noted that institutional policies condemning academic dishonesty are inadequate and insufficient, as problems with cheating occur at the course level, where they may not always be enforced.

Other researchers have identified a number of strategies that institutions and instructors can employ to identify or deter dishonest behavior. Many institutions use a variety of technologies to identify and curtail academic dishonesty, ranging from plagiarism detection software to online proctoring. Others adopt honor codes, although Corrigan-Gibbs, Gupta, Northcutt, Cutrell, and Theis (2015) discovered that general honor codes were not as effective as providing a pre-task warning of the consequences of cheating. To deter cheating at the course level, McGee (2013) proposed a variety of pedagogical strategies that instructors could use to prompt self-awareness and reflection among students, including alternative assessments to reduce their inclination or ability to cheat, such as random quizzes, open-book tests, allowing multiple attempts with the highest score used, and more open-ended assessments, while admitting that such assessments are unlikely to deter students determined to cheat.

If, however, we accept this book's founding premise that we should be listening more to students and exhibiting more care and concern about their experiences and realities, perhaps we should also question some of the solutions proposed to tackle cheating, as well as said solutions' underlying assumptions. More specifically, we should interrogate the assumption behind plagiarism detection and online proctoring software and, by extension, the institutional policies that support them, which is that students are cheating. The technological tools implemented to identify and track cheating rely on monitoring, surveillance, and control, practices that are antithetical to the ideals of progressive education, practices which are potentially insidious and erode trust. As Morris and Stommel (2017) argue, perhaps faculty and administrators should be more critical of these technologies and more trusting of students while crafting activities and assignments that ask students to engage authentically, personally, and deeply with the work. Their position is that rethinking assessment practices will largely address this problem. Ultimately, it is paradoxical to seek developing trusting relationships with our students while asking them, requiring them even, to submit to technologies developed to watch over them.

...

- Academic dishonesty is a growing concern.
- Academic dishonesty perpetuates many harms to individual learners, peers, institutions, and society writ large.
- Factors linked to dishonesty include pressures to succeed, assessment practices, individual students' backgrounds, and so on.
- Some of the solutions and policies aimed at identifying cheating rely on pedagogies of surveillance and control and may erode trust between faculty and students.

References

Barrett, D. 2012. "An Academic Ghostwriter, the 'Shadow Scholar' Comes Clean." *The Chronicle of Higher Education*, August 21. https://www.chronicle.com/article/An-Academic-Ghostwriter-Comes/133904.

Batane, T. 2010. "Turning to Turnitin to Fight Plagiarism among University Students." *Educational Technology & Society* 13 (2): 1–12.

Black, E. W., Greaser, J., and Dawson, K. 2008. "Academic Dishonesty in Traditional and Online Classrooms: Does the 'Media Equation' Hold True?" *Journal of Asynchronous Learning Networks* 12: 23–30.

Corrigan-Gibbs, H., Gupta, N., Northcutt, C., Cutrell, E., and Thies, W. 2015. "Deterring Cheating in Online Environments." *ACM Transactions on Computer-Human Interaction (TOCHI)* 22 (6): 28. http://billthies.net/tochi15-cheating.pdf.

Dante, E. 2010. "The Shadow Scholar: The Man Who Writes Your Students' Papers Tells His Story." *The Chronicle of Higher Education*, November 12. https://www.chronicle.com/.

Fusch, P. I., Ness, L. R., Booker, J. M., and Fusch, G. E. 2017. "The Ethical Implications of Plagiarism and Ghostwriting in an Open Society." *Journal of Social Change* 9 (1): 55–63.

Ison, D. C. 2014. "Does the Online Environment Promote Plagiarism? A Comparative Study of Dissertations from Brick-and-Mortar versus Online Institutions." *Journal of Online Learning and Teaching* 10 (2): 272–282.

Lanier, M. M. 2006. "Academic Integrity and Distance Learning." *Journal of Criminal Justice Education* 17 (2): 244–261.

McGee, P. 2013. "Supporting Academic Honesty in Online Courses." *Journal of Educators Online* 10 (1): 1–31.

Morris, S. M., and Stommel, J. 2017. "A Guide for Resisting EdTech: The Case against Turnitin." *Critical Digital Pedagogy*. https://criticaldigitalpedagogy.pressbooks.com/chapter/a-guide-for-resisting-edtech-the-case-against-turnitin/.

Newton, P. M. 2018. "How Common Is Commercial Contract Cheating in Higher Education and Is It Increasing? A Systematic Review." *Frontiers in Education* (3): 67. doi:10.3389/feduc.2018.00067.

Peled, Y., Eshet, Y., Barczyk, C., and Grinautski, K. 2019. "Predictors of Academic Dishonesty among Undergraduate Students in Online and Face-to-Face Courses." *Computers & Education* 131: 49-59.

Simkin, M. G., and McLeod, A. 2010. "Why Do College Students Cheat?" *Journal of Business Ethics* 94 (3): 441-453.

Watson, G. R., and Sottile, J. 2010. "Cheating in the Digital Age: Do Students Cheat More in Online Courses?" *Online Journal of Distance Learning Administration* 13 (1): 1-13.

11.

The Learner Who Was Taught by a Bot

The narrative that follows is a composite of the experiences of five individuals who had interacted with an intelligent pedagogical agent or a bot. Their experiences are described in more detail in Veletsianos and Miller (2008).

...

I visited Neebin in her office one frigid winter morning to learn about her experiences interacting online with an instructional bot named Jesse. Her office was adorned with plaques of her accomplishments—degrees, awards, pictures—and piled with books and papers everywhere. "Here, have a seat here," she said, removing the papers from a chair and placing them in a neat stack on top of other papers on her desk. After exchanging pleasantries, I quickly got to the crux of my visit: "So, what was it like to have a conversation with a bot?"

At the time, I was studying bots as an instantiation of artificial intelligence (AI). These anthropomorphous digital characters interact with learners and are used in online learning environments to serve various instructional goals through text-to-text and text-to-speech technologies. I was also using a new-to-me interview technique and analytic approach that required asking that sole question and listening intently to the response in order to probe further into Neebin's experience. While some of these interviews were more awkward than others, Neebin was eloquent and descriptive, which made my job of gaining insight into her experience much easier.

"I wanted to know more about this thing," she said, "So, I just started asking Jesse questions such as, 'How are you? What's your name?' I asked questions from popular culture to history and math. We talked about TV shows, about the region where he lived. I felt that I needed to challenge him. I wanted to stump him by asking him difficult, complicated, or misleading questions. . . . I kept on wondering: what else could this thing do?"

As Neebin expected Jesse to respond in human-like ways, she kept asking and asking questions, testing his limits and intelligence. In so doing, she told me, she became "completely engaged" and had no idea how long they talked: "It was like late at night, like three o'clock in the morning, and I was still chatting. . . . I couldn't get up. I was awake, wide awake, and I couldn't get away from my computer." Neebin claimed to be "completely into it," watching, observing, and interacting with the bot while paying little attention to her surroundings. She was describing the kind of educational experience that educational designers aspire to foster: an experience that enthralls learners, pulls them in, and engages them. "I almost forgot where I was," she said. "It is very engrossing." Neebin commented on Jesse's personality, voice, and looks as if he were an actual person, and while his knowledge of the content area that he was enlisted to help with seemed limited at times, she seemed to appreciate and find value in interacting with a rudimentary form of artificial intelligence.

I often ask students in my educational technology courses to debate a variety of issues central to the field. One of my favorite debates revolves around the question of whether teachers should be replaced by AI, which invites students to engage deeply with the work that teachers actually do on a day-to-day basis, as well as with the possibilities and limits of a technology that seems to be concurrently promising and worrisome. Although this debate invites students to imagine teachers being entirely replaced by machines, it is not all that far off the common view that AI offers a promising way to complement and supplement instructional functions, and, indeed, to do away with some of the pesky aspects of what humans bring to teaching. Such a perspective can be seen in Clark's excitement about how AI "holds the promise of high-level teaching that is scalable and cheap" and could be "invaluable for a teaching assistant that never gets tired, inattentive, demotivated, crabby and delivers quality learning experiences, not just answering questions" (2019, para. 12).

Most analyses of the use of AI and bots in digital education focus on effectiveness and efficiency. In particular, proponents of bots and AI often employ the argument that these technologies will enable efficiencies through automation and scalability. In fact, educational technology has historically been envisioned as instilling efficiencies through automation. In 1933, Pressey argued for an "industrial revolution" in education, one "in which educational science and the ingenuity of educational technology combine to modernize the grossly inefficient and clumsy procedures of conventional education" (582). His proposed solution to the inefficiencies of conventional educational practices was a teaching machine, which was a mechanical device that provided learners with a way to respond to information and provided feedback to said input. Nor was Pressey the only one intrigued by the perceived promise of teaching machines: in 1935, Skinner developed his own, the first of which taught arithmetic by asking the student to move a lever to indicate an answer in response to a posed problem and turning on a light when the correct answer was provided.

Among early efforts to standardize, package, and efficiently deliver training to large numbers of people—what some today might call *education at scale*—was the US military's use of audiovisual devices to train a large population of unprepared military personnel and civilians during World War II. While data evaluating the impact of these technologies were not collected, the military's perception at the time was that training films and filmstrips had enabled the United States to efficiently and effectively train these individuals en masse. Despite a similar lack of empirical proof of efficacy, the quest for technologies to deliver training and education at scale has continued through successive waves of technological innovations, including radio and television (Saettler 1990). Even before the advent of the personal computer, content providers such as Encyclopedia Britannica, Disney, and educational institutions invested heavily in information and communication technologies to deliver education via a variety of means and media.

Whereas these early examples used educational technology to make the education of large groups of people more efficient by removing the need for individual instructors to be present, the growing access to computers led many experts in educational technology to shift their focus to developing personalized learning software that tailors instruction to individual learners' needs, skills, and interests. The notion of personalized learning is predicated on defining discrete learning objectives; identifying content to address those objectives; packaging content into discrete chunks; delivering content to individual learners according to various behavioral, emotional, or cognitive measures; and automating the process so that it can be repeated for many different learners in many different contexts. This approach is aligned with the one that imagines using AI to automate education and teaching on a vast scale. In a *Washington Post* article, for example, Basulto (2014) imagined an "artificially intelligent machine" that could teach massive open online courses by "lecturing, grading and engaging with students" and predicted that "once a MOOC can be taught by a machine, it may end up making the delightfully erudite college professor a quaint artifact of the non-digital past"—to his mind, not only a possible future but a desirable one.

The potential of bots—or at least some version of an AI—was reignited in 2016 by Jill Watson, an AI bot powered by IBM's Watson created by Ashok Goel at Georgia Tech to answer questions posed by online students who were not made aware that they would be interacting with a computer. By Goel's account, Jill Watson was so successful at this task that a student posted a message on the discussion board wondering whether Jill Watson was a human or a computer. Although Goel doesn't imagine that bots like Jill will replace human instructors, he does envision that they could free "teaching staff to focus on more creative endeavors" than repeatedly answering the same student questions (TEDx Talks, 2016). Other researchers adopt a more critical perspective, one that aims to resist techno-solutionism, but instead invites educators to "explore how human and non-human teachers might work together in a teaching 'assemblage'" (Bayne 2015, 460). Such an approach resists the use of technology for efficiency's sake and employs it as a course design concept that invites teachers to consider which aspects of their own work may or may not be automated (Bayne, personal communication, February 21, 2017).

Even then, not all commentators are as welcoming of a world with nonhuman teachers and have raised concerns about efforts to automate education instruction. Science fiction writers have warned against dystopian education futures, such as Isaac Asimov's image in *The Fun They Had* (1951) of Margie's future schoolroom, which was right next to her bedroom and housed a mechanical teacher that was always on at the same time and focused solely on lessons, providing little social or emotional support or encouragement. Historian David Noble (1998) also warned against such mechanization and, in particular, against the development and delivery of standardized distance education courses without faculty member participation, which, he argued, would not only degrade learning experiences but commercialize and commodify education through mass production and market logic. Although such concerns may strike some as quaint in an era of interest in upskilling, reskilling, private-public partnerships, education at scale, and online learning, ongoing technological advances make the possibility of automated teaching and assessment ever more likely. While some practitioners imagine a variety of AI technologies reconfiguring the digital learning experience—from using bots to employing hologram lecturers to using automated grading software—others are concerned that such attempts subordinate the social functions of education to its economic imperatives. We face an urgent need to ask probing and difficult questions about the function of education and online learning in relation to automation through AI. While traditional higher education is successful, it leaves many students behind. Is it possible that the automation of various aspects of education may help us broaden access? How do we ensure that such automation not only expands access but does so in a student-centered and caring way? How do we ensure that a future which includes AI is not just a future for those who can't afford education with human teachers?

...

- Proponents of AI and bots argue that such technologies enable automation and efficiencies while liberating faculty to focus on more valuable, creative, and worthwhile activities. This claim is oft-repeated, but some are concerned that the real goal of this effort is to substitute humans with machines.
- Others note that instructor-bot collaboration may be valuable in that it might allow us to consider and develop new pedagogies.

References
Asimov, I. 1951. "The Fun They Had." NEA Service. *Boys and Girls Page*, December 1. http://web1.nbed.nb.ca/sites/ASD-S/1820/J%20Johnston/Isaac%20Asimov%20-%20The%20fun%20they%20had.pdf.

Basulto, D. 2014. "10 Bold Predictions for 2014." *Washington Post*, January 7. http://www.washingtonpost.com/blogs/innovations/wp/2014/01/07/10-bold-predictions-for-2014.

Bayne, S. 2015. "Teacherbot: Interventions in Automated Teaching." *Teaching in Higher Education* 20 (4): 37–41.

Clark, D. 2019. "AI Starts to Crack the Critical Thinking . . . Astonishing Experiment . . ." *Donald Clark Plan B* (blog), March 16. http://donaldclarkplanb.blogspot.com/2019/03/a-champion-debater-has-just-argued-with.html.

Noble, D. 1998. "Digital Diploma Mills: The Automation of Higher Education." *First Monday* 3 (1). https://doi.org/10.5210/fm.v3i1.569.

Pressey, S. 1933. *Psychology and the New Education*. New York: Harper and Bros.

Saettler, P. 1990. *The Evolution of American Educational Technology.* Greenwich, CT: Information Age Publishing.

TEDx Talks. 2016. *A Teaching Assistant Named Jill Watson | Ashok Goel. TEDxSanFrancisco.* YouTube video, posted November 1. https:// www.youtube.com/watch?v=WbCguICyfTA.

Veletsianos, G., and Miller, C. 2008. "Conversing with Pedagogical Agents: A Phenomenological Exploration of Interacting with Digital Entities." *British Journal of Educational Technology* 39 (6): 969–986.

12.

The Learner Who Took Notes

My colleague Dr. Amy Collier interviewed Luis, and the interview with him began like all the rest, with an exchange of pleasantries and an attempt to confirm that the technology they were using was working well. After a couple of tries and a bit of tweaking, Amy began her conversation with Luis, a 25-year-old El Salvadorian, on the other end of her webcam.

Like many young people, Luis had gone to university without being entirely sure what he wanted to do with his life. In the back of his mind, he had always toyed with the idea of attending culinary school. Since he was a young boy, he had felt a connection to cooking. His parents had often worked late when Luis was growing up, so he frequently needed to cook for himself. Rather than view his time in the kitchen as a chore, however, he had found it empowering and entertaining, an opportunity to draw on his creative and artistic talents. But his university studies had seemed to take him further and further from his dream of culinary school, and the more time he spent in lecture halls, the more he began to feel there were no viable career paths for him there. At the time of the interview, he was exploring his appetite for the culinary arts: he had already completed one open online course and was enrolled in three others—a nutrition course, a child nutrition course, and a healthy eating course. He had also made the decision to drop out of university and follow his passion.

When asked what practices he found useful in completing his online studies, Luis said he took notes. Although he may not have learned a great deal about cooking in university, he had learned quite a bit about the value of note-taking: "Writing things down helps me focus on what's important," he said, "it helps me remember." Holding up a blue notebook, he said that he would use it to write notes while completing course quizzes, watching lecture videos, and reading transcripts. Sometimes he would pause the videos to carefully pen notes on what he had heard. Other times, he might sit back with his notebook on his lap and jot down words or phrases while the video was playing. When there was a lot of text on the screen and no transcript was available, he said, he would often take a screenshot and save it to a file dedicated to the course. Often, he would then print out the image and clip it to a page in his notebook.

The video streaming from Luis's webcam allowed Amy to follow along as he illustrated his points by flipping through his notes. Multicolored notes, highlighted text, and hastily drawn sketches covered the pages from bound edge to tattered edge. He read aloud some of the headings in his notes, which included "Tips for preserving vitamins," "Determining proteins in micronutrients," "Dietary sources of fat," and "Financial cost of obesity." "At least I think that's what that last one says," he added, laughing and pointing to where his coffee mug had left a brown ring across the page.

If Luis had chosen to take his notes using his computer, they might not have suffered the indignity of being used as a coaster, but Luis said he enjoyed the exercise of putting pen to paper. He liked to write and draw, and used note-taking as a break from staring at the screen. He also found writing on paper helpful for studying and sharing: "I believe it's better for me to write it in a notebook because when I go out, if I have time, I can read it. I can share it with my friend or with someone in the gym." And as a non-native English speaker, Luis also used his notes as an opportunity to practice the language and to work on his reading and writing skills; another reason he found it invaluable to have his notebook near him at all times.

As the interview wrapped up, he closed his notebook, its binding bulging to accommodate the crowded pages. He would clearly need a new notebook when starting culinary school next fall.

•••

Online learning requires numerous skills and literacies, including time management, effective reading strategies, and critical thinking skills, and a variety of literacies, some of which were explored in chapter 6. Among these, nearly every student my colleagues and I interviewed over the last four years, and nearly every student I've ever taught, took notes in one form or another. In the study upon which this chapter is based (Veletsianos, Collier, and Schneider 2015) some learners reported that their notes stemmed primarily from lectures, while others described using notes to record comments from discussion forums or conversations they had with peers in other settings. Many learners mentioned taking notes on their readings or to add information to their lecture notes. Others noted that they would sometimes pause a lecture video to take notes because they wanted to think some more about the topic or to jot down a particular idea or point they wanted to return to in the future. Some learners even described complex note-taking strategies that they had developed, such as combining notes across multiple courses, collaboratively taking notes with peers using co-writing technologies such as Google Documents, or arranging their notes in certain ways to use them in their exams or future studies.

While Luis's well-used and ever-present notebook was by no means unique, the tools used to take notes and the subsequent uses of those notes tended to vary substantially among learners. Some of these learners would take notes on paper, whether in notebooks designated for the course, in more general journals they carried with them at all times, or on loose sheets of paper they would later organize by course or by topic. Other learners reported taking notes digitally. Often those learners used word processing software to type notes or, like Luis, took screenshots when a lot of information was presented. Some would also clip excerpts from the digital materials themselves by copying and pasting text from the video lecture transcripts into their notes or would take notes directly on PDFs of the presenters' slides. Other learners took both paper and digital notes, combining formats in a variety of ways to meet their individual needs. One student, for instance, told me, "I have a ring-bound notebook, and I make quite neat notes if I can. [They are] probably totally illegible, but to me they look neat. And I also have a ring file folder. And then I have some [notes] on my hard disk, [where] I keep some folders [with notes] as well."

While an early study noted that writing things down by hand (as opposed to typing) seems to improve retention (Mueller and Oppenheimer 2014), a replication study failed to generate the same findings (Morehead, Dunlosky, and Rawson 2019). The choice of whether to take digital or paper notes in our study largely seemed to be a personal preference that was influenced by how the learners planned to use their notes in the future. Luis, for example, preferred taking notes on paper because doing so gave him a break from staring at the screen and because he could carry them with him to reference and share anytime and anywhere. Others used their digital course notes as the foundation for writing assignments. They described rereading their notes, adding key points, and synthesizing concepts presented in the course with their own ideas. Having notes in digital form seemed to make it easier for some students to produce a final piece of digitized writing.

A perhaps less expected response was that learners mentioned sharing their notes with others as frequently as using notes to support studying, taking quizzes, or doing writing assignments. Note-taking, therefore, may have a role to play in building learning communities, through such practices as sharing of notes or collaborative note-taking. Several learners also planned to use their notes for personal and professional purposes after their courses were over. One student for instance, shared that "what I wrote down is more for how I can apply what's in the course to the work that I'm doing in my job right now." Another student reported that "these two or three classes are pretty relevant to the information that I need for the Childcare Center, [so] I plan on going back and reusing them."

Note-taking, whether in online or face-to-face courses, is widely considered an essential and sophisticated study skill, as it allows learners to create a document for later reference and to deepen their understanding through a personal articulation of topics (Kobayashi 2005). To encourage note-taking, digital learning platforms could be designed to integrate note-taking tools that would support the note-taking process in multiple ways. The platform could scaffold that process, for example, or instructors could provide templates that would direct learners' attention to types of information that they would benefit from writing down or to model particular note-taking strategies that have proven beneficial in other contexts, such as creating concept maps or reframing concepts and information in their own words.

Another potential advantage of integrating note-taking in digital platforms is that it could allow learners to write notes individually or collaboratively. Collaborative note-taking has been found to be a powerful strategy for leveraging the collective knowledge and interest of a group of learners (Kam et al. 2005; Steimle, Brdiczka, and Muhlhauser 2008; Miyake and Masukawa 2000). A note-taking system integrated into a platform could also incorporate capabilities beyond the traditional linear organization of paper notes or text files (Schneider 2014), such as connecting notes to particular moments in a video or assessments in the form of annotations or notes on the resources themselves. Notes could be tagged (automatically or by the student) by the concepts the notes are covering, which would make retrieval easier for studying and later reference.

Based on my research, it seems that many learners often see their notes as deeply personal creations that are meaningful to them. Luis considered his notebook not only a practical tool but a source of pride. He had created something useful and enduring, something that demonstrated how much he had learned, tailored to his own preferences and needs, and something that he was eager to share with others. So, although incorporating note-taking affordances into digital platforms would support valuable pedagogical practices, learners should also be given ownership over their notes, both in the process of their creation and in continued access to the artifacts they create. Tools to support digital note-taking, therefore, should embrace an ethos of student ownership and enable learners to make use of their notes across platforms and devices. Students should be able to export the notes they create in a variety of different formats for easy sharing, retrieval, and reuse. Such a system would support, respect, and empower learners to take and organize their notes to fit their needs, including making connections in that information across multiple courses and platforms.

To be certain, this argument is aimed at more than just notes and note-taking: subscription-based business models, including textbook rentals and digital homework systems, often rely on "access" rather than ownership. And students rarely, if ever, *own* or have control over the data they leave behind as they participate in digital learning platforms. That data in particular become resources for educational technology companies and are often sold back to universities and students in the form of algorithms and software. Any approach to online education that is learner-centered needs to engage with these ideas and, at the very least, investigate what data are collected about students from the platforms they are asked to use, how that data is being used, whether students can opt-out, and for how long that data are maintained before being deleted.

...

- Students take notes on paper or digitally for a variety of reasons and in a variety of ways, sometimes sharing those notes with others or organizing them in unique ways that support their studies.

- Instructors and digital learning platforms can support learners' efforts by scaffolding note-taking.
- Student agency and ownership over their notes—and textbooks, data, and other class materials—is an important issue that necessitates greater attention.

References

Kam, M., Wang, J., Iles, A., Tse, E., Chiu, J., Glaser, D., Tarshish, O., and Canny, J. 2005. "Livenotes: A System for Cooperative and Augmented Note-Taking in Lectures." In *Proceedings of the SIGCHI Conference on Human Factors in Computing Systems*, 531–540. New York: ACM.

Kobayashi, K. 2005. "What Limits the Encoding Effect of Note-Taking? A Meta-analytic Examination." *Contemporary Educational Psychology* 30 (2): 242–262.

Miyake, N., and Masukawa, H. 2000. "Relation-Making to Sense-Making: Supporting College Students' Constructive Understanding with an Enriched Collaborative Note-Sharing System." In *Fourth International Conference of the Learning Sciences*, edited by B. Fishman and S. O'Connor-Divelbiss, 41–47. Mahwah, NJ: Erlbaum.

Morehead, K., Dunlosky, J., and Rawson, K. A. 2019. "How Much Mightier Is the Pen Than the Keyboard for Note-Taking? A Replication and Extension of Mueller and Oppenheimer." *Educational Psychology Review*: 1–28.

Mueller, P. A., and Oppenheimer, D. M. 2014. "The Pen Is Mightier Than the Keyboard: Advantages of Longhand over Laptop Note Taking." *Psychological Science* 25 (6): 1159–1168.

Schneider, E. 2014. "Designing a Hyperlearning Annotation Tool." In *Proceedings of the Learning Innovations at Scale Workshop*, CHI. http://lytics.stanford.edu/wp-content/ uploads/2014/08/chi -annotation-short-paper.pdf.

Steimle, J., Brdiczka, O., and Mühlhäuser, M. 2008. "CoScribe: Using Paper for Collaborative Annotations in Lectures." n.p.: IEEE. In *2008 Eighth IEEE International Conference on Advanced Learning Technologies*, 306–310. http://dx.doi.org/10.1109/ICALT.2008.39.

13.

The Learner Who Used a Social Networking Site for Online Learning

When I talked to Maxine, she had just completed her third online course. The first two had been writing courses that "just [involved] a string of assignments" and mostly required her to write papers, send them to peers, critique papers she received, revise her own papers, and submit them to the instructor. The third course was different. It encompassed "a whole lot more interaction" through a different kind of platform, a social networking site.

But social media was a foreign concept to Maxine. Before the course, she "had never used Facebook or MySpace or any of that stuff," and even though she had watched videos on YouTube, she had never uploaded one of her own there or contributed any other content to the internet for broad consumption. As a graduate student and mother of three, two of whom were still teenagers living at home, Maxine also had little time for social media. She felt overwhelmed, nervous, and "really scared" when, on the first day of her third online course, she was informed that the course made use of a social networking site through which she would have to write blog posts and connect with others in a more social way than that afforded to students via typical online learning platforms. "I didn't know how to post information or friend people or anything like that," she told me. At the age of 39, Maxine was apprehensive about social media because she was "just kind of afraid of the different privacy issues and who does the content that you put on there really belongs to."

As time went by, though, she felt "more protected," having realized that the site had been created solely for the group consisting of herself, her peers, and their instructor. Maxine also decided that she was not going to post anything on this site that wasn't related to the class, a decision that made her feel more comfortable. The longer she was in the course, the more the technology started making sense to her. She saw its use as "making the most of all the tools that we had and using them as tools to support our learning." She even enlisted the help of her 12-year-old daughter to hold the camera to record a video and made sure to keep her on track: "She was playing with the focus and all those sort of things," she said laughing, and by the time she was able to complete her assignment, "it ended up being sometime after midnight." A number of factors thus mitigated the challenges and risks of the social networking platform that she was using, including the fact that it was not a public social media site and that the course seemed to make appropriate pedagogical use of it.

...

Online education has traditionally been organized, supported, and delivered through Learning Management Systems (LMS) such as Canvas, Blackboard, and Moodle, which draw together a variety of technologies that enable institutions and instructors to provide a structured, efficient, and secure learning experience (West, Waddoups, and Graham 2006; DeSchryver et al. 2009; Lee and McLoughlin 2010;). Such systems serve as one-stop locations for students to engage in a variety of activities, ranging from retrieving a syllabus to engaging in peer discussions to viewing course grades. Despite these platforms' many benefits, a number of researchers have argued that they have generally been used as static repositories of content rather than providing the kinds of rich social experiences found on digital platforms of the likes of Facebook, Instagram, and YouTube (Brady et al. 2010; Lee and McLoughlin 2010; Schroeder, Minocha, and Schneider 2010; Whitworth and Benson 2010). LMS have also been criticized for suppressing student motivation and enthusiasm (DeSchryver et al. 2009; Naveh, Tubin, and Pliskin 2010) and inhibiting pedagogical innovation through their default settings and familiar features (Lane 2009).

As a result, about a decade ago, educators and researchers began exploring alternative platforms to provide learners with social communication tools that could improve ease of use, pedagogical freedom, fluid online discussions, and identity management (Webb 2009, Brady et al. 2010; Lee and McLoughlin 2010). Some faculty and course designers began to appropriate popular social media tools for use in higher education because of the perceived opportunities and benefits they present for improving pedagogical practices and student engagement. Instructors have employed these tools by asking students to reflect on their learning in blogs, contribute to publicly available resources such as Wikipedia, connect with communities of interest through LinkedIn and Reddit, and participate on a variety of other platforms that exemplify the "read-and-write" ethos of the contemporary internet. At the core of these participatory practices is the internet's ability to provide users with opportunities to contribute, consume, share, and remix content (Greenhow, Robelia, and Hughes 2009).

The educational technology literature on the use of social media has investigated a wide range of topics, including both students' and faculty's attitudes toward, use of, and experiences with social media. This research has shown, for example, that although faculty members increasingly appear to use social media for scholarly purposes (Veletsianos 2016), they seem more cautious about adopting them for instructional purposes. Ajjan and Hartshorne (2008) found that 74% of the faculty they studied did not plan on using social networking tools for instruction; Coddington (2010) reported that 79% of approximately 4,600 faculty surveyed had never used collaborative editing software (e.g., wikis) and 84% had never used blogs in their teaching; and Roblyer et al. (2010) uncovered that higher education faculty seemed more inclined to use more traditional technologies, such as email. Although such findings might appear to suggest that faculty unfamiliarity and resistance is primarily responsible for the limited use of social media for instructional purposes in higher education, Ajjan and Hartshorne argue that the larger reason is that such tools are incompatible with the way that higher education is generally organized and delivered. In particular, they point to important structural and philosophical differences between how participatory technologies such as social media envision the relationships between participants and how higher education institutions envision the relationships between faculty and students. For instance, whereas social media tends to collapse hierarchical structures, the higher education classroom has traditionally valued the voice of a single expert (i.e., the faculty member). This explanation is consistent with Coddington's finding that, despite the low social media use they uncovered among surveyed faculty, 72% of those faculty members used course management systems such as Blackboard, which generally support instructor-centric learning environments.

Despite the common view among proponents in the field that social media can be useful in addressing problems that have traditionally plagued distance education, such as a lack of interaction between participants, there is still a paucity of research examining student experiences with social media in online courses. In a study of students' experiences using a social network in a blended course, Arnold and Paulus (2010) found that students believed that the social networking features of the site encouraged community-building and that the public nature of the tasks allowed for modeling and feedback. The authors also observed that students may have also engaged in additional learning activities that were invisible to the researchers, such as reading other students' entries without responding to them (see chapter 9). In a study of an online undergraduate course, Dron and Anderson (2009) reported that learners in their course had a generally positive learning experience but sometimes also got "lost in social space" and needed support and scaffolding from the instructor to effectively participate in the social network. In our own investigations, we discovered similar patterns: though students enjoyed and appreciated the social learning experience, they limited their participation to course-related activities and devised strategies to manage the expansive amount of information generated through the social space in order to focus on the activities that they deemed most valuable to their learning (Veletsianos and Navarrete 2012).

While education researchers have generally been hopeful about the positive impact of social media on education, others have been more skeptical about its actual educational benefits (e.g., Manca and Ranieri 2013; Selwyn and Stirling 2016). Selwyn (2009), for example, dismissed the kind of learning that occurred in a study of undergraduates' naturally occurring Facebook interactions as representing the "chatter of the back row of the lecture hall" (170). Schroeder et al. (2010) also offered a long list of potential concerns that may arise when using social software in higher education, including workload concerns for faculty and students, lack of trust in peer feedback, ownership issues with regard to social media spaces, and difficulties in adapting publicly available tools and protecting the anonymity of students. Furthermore, Madge, Meek, Wellens, and Hooley (2009) have suggested that social networking sites might be more useful for informal rather than formal learning, as 91% of the undergraduates in their study had never used such tools to communicate with university staff and 43% believed that SNSs have no potential for academic work. Beyond these concerns, others point to ongoing scandals and concerns facing technology companies in recent years (e.g., Facebook and Cambridge Analytica, the possibility of YouTube's recommendation algorithm favoring extremism, Twitter's ongoing failure to address harassment), and wonder whether these online environments are hospitable for learning.

Like many technologies, social media may be a useful part of a toolkit in designing effective online learning. While some evidence seems to suggest that social media can be an effective pedagogical tool, enabling such synergistic activities as collaboration, social interaction, reflective practice, situated learning, and authentic assessment, we need to approach them with an ethic of care and consider that adopting these technologies in our courses means inviting their business practices and their ideologies in our classrooms.

. . .

- The flat organizational structure of social media may be incompatible with the traditionally hierarchical structure of the classroom. In this respect, social media technologies are congruent with progressive pedagogical approaches that value social interaction and participation.
- Researchers have generally been hopeful about the role of social media in online learning. Nonetheless, the learning that happens on social media most often seems more fitting for informal learning settings.
- An emerging tension around the use of social media in education revolves around the question of whether the environments fostered and cultivated by technology companies are hospitable for learning.

References

Ajjan, H., and Hartshorne, R. 2008. "Investigating Faculty Decisions to Adopt Web 2.0 Technologies: Theory and Empirical Tests." *Internet and Higher Education* 11 (2): 71–80.

Arnold, N., and Paulus, T. 2010. "Using a Social Networking Site for Experiential Learning: Appropriating, Lurking, Modeling and Community Building." *Internet and Higher Education* 11 (2): 71–80.

Brady, K. P., Holcomb, L. B., and Smith, B. V. 2010. "The Use of Alternative Social Networking Sites in Higher Educational Settings: A Case Study of the e-Learning Benefits of Ning in Education." *Journal of Interactive Online Learning* 9 (2): 151–170.

Coddington, R. 2010. "Professors' Use of Technology in Teaching." *The Chronicle of Higher Education*, July 25. http://chronicle.com/article/article-content/123682/.

DeSchryver, M., Mishra, P., Koehleer, M., and Francis, A. 2009. "Moodle vs. Facebook: Does Using Facebook for Discussions in an Online Course Enhance Perceived Social Presence and Student Interaction?" In *Proceedings of Society for Information Technology &*

Teacher Education International Conference, edited by I. Gibson, R. Weber, K. McFerrin, R. Carlsen & D. Willis, 329–336. Charleston, SC: Association for the Advancement of Computing in Education.

Dron, J., and Anderson, T. 2009. "Lost in Social Space: Information Retrieval Issues in Web1.5." *Journal of Digital Information* 10 (2): 1–12.

Greenhow, C. G., Robelia, B., and Hughes, J. 2009. "Learning, Teaching, and Scholarship in a Digital Age Web 2.0 and Classroom Research: What Path Should We Take Now?" *Educational Researcher* 38 (4): 246–259.

Lane, L. 2009. "Insidious Pedagogy: How Course Management Systems Impact Teaching." *First Monday* 14 (10).

Lee, M. J. W., and McLoughlin, C. 2010. "Beyond Distance and Time Constraints: Applying Social Networking Tools and Web 2.0 Approaches to Distance Learning." In *Emerging Technologies in Distance Education*, 61–87. Edmonton: Athabasca University Press.

Madge, C., Meek, J., Wellens, J., and Hooley, T. 2009. "Facebook, Social Integration and Informal Learning at University: 'It Is More for Socialising and Talking to Friends about Work Than for Actually Doing Work.'" *Learning, Media and Technology* 34 (2): 141.

Manca, S., and Ranieri, M. 2013. "Is It a Tool Suitable for Learning? A Critical Review of the Literature on Facebook as a Technology-Enhanced Learning Environment." *Journal of Computer Assisted Learning* 29 (6): 487–504.

Naveh, G., Tubin, D., and Pliskin, N. 2010. "Student LMS Use and Satisfaction in Academic Institutions: The Organizational Perspective." *Internet and Higher Education* 13 (3): 127–133.

Roblyer, M., McDaniel, M., Webb, M., Herman, J., and Witty, J. V. 2010. "Findings on Facebook in Higher Education: A Comparison of College Faculty and Student Uses and Perceptions of Social Networking Sites." *Internet and Higher Education* 13 (3): 134–140.

Schroeder, A., Minocha, S., and Schneider, C. 2010. "The Strengths, Weaknesses, Opportunities and Threats of Using Social Software in Higher and Further Education Teaching and Learning." *Journal of Computer Assisted Learning* 26 (3): 159–174.

Selwyn, N. 2009. "Faceworking: Exploring Students' Education-Related Use of 'Facebook.'" *Learning, Media and Technology* 34 (2): 157–174.

Selwyn, N., and Stirling, E. 2016. "Social Media and Education . . . Now the Dust Has Settled." *Learning, Media and Technology* 41 (1): 1–5.

Veletsianos, G. 2016. *Networked Scholars: Social Media in Academia.* New York: Routledge.

Veletsianos, G., and Navarrete, C. 2012. "Online Social Networks as Formal Learning Environments: Learner Experiences and Activities." *International Review of Research in Open and Distance Learning* 13 (1): 144–166.

Webb, E. 2009. "Engaging Students with Engaging Tools." *Educause Quarterly* 32 (4): 1–7.

West, R., Waddoups, G., and Graham, C. 2006. "Understanding the Experiences of Instructors as They Adopt a Course Management System." *Educational Technology Research and Development* 55 (1): 1–26.

Whitworth, A., and Benson, A. 2010. "Learning, Design, and Emergence: Two Cases of Moodle in Distance Education." In *Emerging Technologies in Distance Education*, 195–213. Edmonton: Athabasca University Press.

14.

The Learner Who Was Self-Directed

Due to fortuitously coinciding travel plans, Gwen was one of a few online learners discussed in this volume whom my research assistant was able to interview in person. Gwen had described herself as a "total tech geek" and an experienced and accomplished online learner, with nearly as many MOOCs under her belt as credentials following her email signature. She described herself as "your typical nana" and when my research assistant saw a smiling and furiously knitting woman with long, silver hair at the quaint English coffeehouse they agreed to meet, she knew she had found her.

Asked to describe her background, the 62-year-old educator reported, "I've been a primary school teacher, a special needs education teacher, a school leader, headteacher for a number of years. Now I've moved into higher ed, and I'm teaching teachers." She paused to corral several wayward balls of yarn and stuffed them in her backpack. "Most of my own learning, back in the 'olden days,' was very traditional—classroom, lecture sort of stuff. And then I did my master's course."

Her master's course in educational technology, taken through a university several hundred miles away from the Scottish town where she lived, was Gwen's first experience with online learning. "It was . . . I shouldn't say laissez-faire, but just that sense of you're in charge of your own learning and you have to make out of it what you can." After completing her master's, Gwen continued on to complete a doctorate, which was also done mainly online. "You had to be very comfortable with not knowing where you're going or what you're doing. And you had to figure it out yourself."

These experiences drew Gwen to MOOCs, which she had learned about from a colleague in her PhD cohort. "They fit my style of learning," she explained. Her first course was a MOOC in social psychology through Coursera, but "I think I lasted about three weeks," she said laughingly. "I don't know why I signed up. It was a month before I had to submit my thesis, and I'd just started a new job." Undaunted by this first experience, however, Gwen continued on, participating in, by her best guess, 20 MOOCs over the previous three years.

"They're all very different," she reflected. "The psychology one was glossy," by which she meant "they'd obviously run this thing loads of times, they'd had thousands of people. It was following a well-trodden path, which was a bit of a yawn, a bit boring. But that's not always a bad thing. There are times when that's absolutely appropriate and that's what you want as a student." To illustrate that point, she reported, "I did a course in corpus linguistics last year and that's exactly what I wanted; it was totally new to me, and I wanted to see how this particular world expert goes about teaching this. And it was 'here's what you do Week 1, 2, 3,' with little quizzes so I could test my comprehension."

But the free-form scarf flying off her knitting needles suggested that linear structures weren't always her thing. Her eyes lit up as she described a course that was exploratory, that included "just volume of stuff—people, postings, creating things" and encompassed "no right answers, no structured direction," a course where "you really had to figure out what you wanted to get out of it by yourself." When asked how she navigated this "volume of stuff," she replied, "I went through pretty much everybody's blogs and I read a lot. And then I had to walk away and leave it for a bit, let things sift through. And once I knew I could walk away, I could come back, I didn't have to be there all the time, online all the time, I was okay." She offered the following advice for other students discovering online courses or MOOCs:

> You need a reason for doing this, sure, but you also need confidence. You need to be fairly happy with . . . not lack of structure, necessarily . . . finding your own path, your own route. So, you need to know what you're looking for. You need to be someone who is really curious, the kind of person that thinks "I wonder what will happen if I press this button?" sort of thing. And then you also have to be willing and able to sit back and say "yeah, I pressed this button and it all exploded. Now what have I learned from that?" Which is quite hard.

This process can be difficult, and some students may find it too daunting, too chaotic. But certain kinds of curious, self-directed learners are likely to find that aspect of learning online valuable. In fact, Gwen noted, "That's what I love about the online environment. You can dip in and experience and see that there are multiple ways of doing things and make your own choices about what you need at this time."

· · ·

For the most part, the learning that takes place online in informal settings or open online courses entails a large degree of independence and autonomy. In contrast, in typical educational settings, curricula and instructors structure and guide the learning experience. Though this difference might imply that learners in informal settings may require a different skillset than those in formal settings, self-directed learning skills are increasingly emphasized for any individual participating in an online program—not just for completing the program but because such skills can prove useful on a lifelong basis as individuals continue to apply them to their learning. Downes' observation that "MOOCs expect that their participants will be motivated and will have learned how to learn" (2012, para. 12) applies equally to any online course. And while some students, like Gwen, may be clearly skilled and experienced in directing their own learning pathways, others can struggle and might need more assistance in navigating the complex process of self-directed learning.

Self-directed learning, as described by Knowles, is "a process in which individuals take the initiative, with or without the help of others, in diagnosing their learning needs, formulating learning goals, identifying human and material resources for learning, choosing and implementing appropriate learning strategies, and evaluating learning outcomes" (1975, 18). While theories and models of self-directed learning have existed for a long time, the rise of online learning has brought renewed interest to the topic. As Song and Hill (2007) have identified, there are three dimensions that contribute to one's ability to direct their own learning: personal attributes (e.g., experience, knowledge, access to resources, motivations), processes engaged in while learning (e.g., learners' planning their time, evaluating resources and information, monitoring their comprehension), and learning contexts (e.g., learning activities, availability of support). Self-directed learning skills that successful learners draw upon include their ability to manage and plan their time, cope with vast amounts of information by choosing what to focus on, and use a variety of tools and resources both inside and outside of the course platform to support their learning (Kop and Fournier 2011; Waite, Mackness, Roberts, and Lovegrove 2013; Beaven et al. 2014). Having prior experience in similar online learning environments, particularly ones that require participants to draw upon self-directed learning skills, has been shown to contribute to successful participation (Milligan, Littlejohn and Margaryan 2013; de Waard, Kukulska-Hulme, and Sharples 2015).

Central to these skills is the emphasis on personal agency and self-efficacy (Ryan and Deci 2000). Indeed, Bonk and Lee (2017) note that participants' being able to set their own learning goals and to successfully direct their own learning increased their confidence, self-efficacy, and self-worth, which then helped them meet their learning goals. Recognizing that learner autonomy is central to success in online learning helps highlight some of the skills and competencies that educational institutions, instructors, and designers should expect students to have or to acquire and thus support with structures or educational initiatives. A number of institutions seek to help students determine whether they are appropriate candidates for such courses through online learning readiness assessments, which highlight behaviors and attitudes that are closely tied to self-directed learning. Such assessments for instance, ask learners to evaluate whether they can minimize distractions, monitor their progress, plan effectively, assess their progress, and engage in a number of other self-directed behaviors/skills.

Although scholars and institutions recognize that online learning requires these skills, they tend to put the onus on students to gain them on their own rather than design their programs and instruction to teach and nurture them. In other words, learners are *expected* to be self-directed, autonomous, and know how to learn. Though this expectation may appear innocuous, online learning that expects learners to possess these skills leaves behind the learners who potentially stand to benefit the most; the learners who do not already possess such skills.

Gwen's narrative demonstrates how the traits that are common among self-determined learners helped her succeed. She described drawing upon a number of self-regulated learning and metacognitive skills, such as monitoring her learning, checking that she understood the meaning of a task, and setting personal learning goals. As researchers have found, however, a lack of unfamiliarity with online environments—particularly with the complex and often distributed environment of courses that depend on technologies beyond Learning Management Systems—can lead to confusion, disorientation, stress, and anxiety that negatively affect a learner's learning, confidence, desire to pursue further learning experiences, and belief in one's self-efficacy (McAuley et al. 2010; Milligan, Littlejohn, and Margaryan 2013). Online students who are more familiar with online tools and contexts are able to spend less time searching for information and more time engaging in effective learning strategies (Song and Hill 2007). As an experienced online learner, when Gwen took the course in corpus linguistics—a topic in which she had little prior knowledge—she didn't have to devote any of her time or cognitive resources to learning how to use the technologies and learning environment and could instead concentrate on such learning processes as planning her time and activities and monitoring her comprehension to help her better understand the new material. Her experience also illustrates the importance of motivation in self-determined learning. As she noted at the end of the interview, "You need to have a goal" for your participation. Gwen seems to have intrinsically understood the connection that Beaven et al. (2014) found between clear goals, confidence, motivation, persistence, and successful engagement.

When Gwen spoke about the exploratory course she experienced, it was easy to tell it had been her favorite experience to that point. It was a highly unstructured course, one that focused on discussing, creating, and connecting with others. This type of course, Beaven et al. (2014) suggest, requires an even higher level of self-determination than content-based courses, as participants who are not highly motivated or who struggle to gain support from peers will find it difficult to succeed. Even with her extensive experience and high level of self-directed learning skills, Gwen still felt initially overwhelmed with the "volume" of the course. She tried using strategies like engaging deeply with the content by "reading everyone's blog," but eventually it was her sense of autonomy in being able to step away from the course and to engage on her own terms that led to increased confidence in herself and to her "being okay" with the design of the course.

The self-determined learners who succeed in online learning experiences typically possess traits such as persistence, independence, self-confidence, and an enjoyment of learning. They are curious, willing to try new things, and resilient if and when things "explode." The time and effort put into mastering these skills can allow students like Gwen to "dip in and experience" a variety of different online learning options and "make your [their] choices about what [they] need at this time." For Gwen, learning had become not just the means to an end, but a goal in itself.

...

- Self-directed learning skills are a central component of online learning.
- Institutions should foster and support the development of such skills in all learners.

References

Beaven, T., Hauck, M., Coman-Quinn, A., Lewis, T., and de los Arcos, B. 2014. "MOOCs: Striking the Right Balance between Facilitation and Self-Determination." *MERLOT Journal of Online Learning and Teaching* 10 (1): 31–43.

Bonk, C. J., and Lee, M. M. 2017. "Motivations, Achievements, and Challenges of Self-Directed Informal Learners in Open Educational Environments and MOOCs." *Journal of Learning for Development* 4 (1): 36–57.

de Waard, I., Kukulska-Hulme, A., and Sharples, M. 2015. "Self-Directed Learning in Trial FutureLearn Courses." In *Proceedings Papers*, 234–243. n.p., UK: EMOOCS. http://oro.open.ac.uk/44499 /1/eMOOCs-2015_submission_65.pdf.

Downes, S. 2012. "What a MOOC Does." *Stephen's Web* (blog), March 1. http://downes.ca/post/57728.

Knowles, M. S. 1975. *Self-Directed Learning.* New York: Association Press.

Kop, R., and Fournier, H. 2011. "New Dimensions to Self-Directed Learning in an Open Networked Learning Environment." *International Journal of Self-Directed Learning* 7 (2): 1–18.

McAuley, A., Stewart, B., Siemens, G., and Cormier, D. 2010. *The MOOC Model for Digital Practice.* Charlottetown: University of Prince Edward Island. https://oerknowledgecloud.org/sites /oerknowledgecloud.org/files/MOOC_Final.pdf.

Milligan, C., Littlejohn, A., and Margaryan, A. 2013. "Patterns of Engagement in Connectivist MOOCs." *Journal of Online Learning & Teaching* 9 (2): 149–159.

Ryan, R. M., and Deci, E. L. 2000. "Self-Determination Theory and the Facilitation of Intrinsic Motivation, Social Development, and Well-Being." *American Psychologist* 55 (1): 68–78.

Song, L., and Hill, J. R. 2007. "A Conceptual Model for Understanding Self-Directed Learning in Online Environments." *Journal of Interactive Online Learning* 6 (1): 27–42.

Waite, M., Mackness, J., Roberts, G., and Lovegrove, E. 2013. "Liminal Participants and Skilled Orienteers: Learner Participation in a MOOC for New Lecturers." *Journal of Online Learning and Teaching* 9 (2). http://jolt.merlot.org/vol9no2/waite_0613.htm.

15.

The Learner Who Took Advantage of the Openness in MOOCs

Mary and her demanding Pomeranian, Becca, live deep in the heart of Texas. Exclaiming "I have a passion for the law!" when I called her on her landline, the 34-year-old Austin resident told us she had once seriously considered going to law school and had even aced her LSAT, the law school entrance exam used by universities in the United States. But after finishing four intense years earning a bachelor's degree, she had decided to wait a bit. "Law school just didn't seem like a good choice at the time," she reflected. Five years later, Mary had settled into her work as a business consultant. Although her interest in the law was still keen and she'd never completely given up the dream of law school, it had been tempered with a bit of realism. "I don't know if I can afford to spend another three years in the classroom," she confided, and "I don't know if I still have the same passion for the legal industry as I did five years ago."

Mary had first learned about MOOCs during a hot afternoon enjoying frozen mango margaritas with a friend and shortly thereafter signed up for a number of courses, dabbling in some and promptly forgetting about others. One day, an ad for ContractsX, a course on contract law taught by a Harvard professor, popped up on her screen and she decided to "give it a shot." What did she have to lose? "It's a free class, taught at one of the more well-respected institutions—why not?" she added with a laugh.

The course was flexible and fit into her busy life. On Saturday mornings, she told us, she would sit in her office with Becca by her side and a warm cup of dark roast coffee in her hand and watch the Harvard law lectures on her trusted iPad. These weren't just any lectures, however; Professor Fried was an engaging storyteller, a master of his trade who used short, interesting, and memorable stories to teach concepts related to contract law. "I can't believe that I'm sitting here," Mary recalled thinking, "learning this material from Harvard Law!" The fast-paced content made the course challenging, Mary acknowledged, and she didn't always do as well as she would have liked on the quizzes. But because she was able to go back to review the answers and re-watch the videos, this didn't worry her too much, and she ended up passing the course with flying colors. Proud of her certificate of accomplishment, Mary reported that her success in the course "makes me want to keep coming back for more!"

Even though it was a personal rather than professional interest in the law that led Mary to sign up for this course, she found what she learned in the course was helpful when dealing with contracts in her own job and had enthusiastically recommended the course to coworkers and friends. She was currently taking a number of other open courses and was anxiously awaiting the second version of the contracts course. As a result of the course, Mary's self-confidence had increased: "I never thought of applying to Harvard. There was no way I would be getting in. But then, five years later, I'm taking a course from Harvard. I wouldn't say that I'm a Harvard law student, but at least now I could sit across from a Harvard law student and have a clear conversation with them. It's very rewarding to know that."

...

Mary's passion for the law came through loud and clear in her story. But even though she would have loved to pursue a law degree, she considered the cost and time required prohibitive and worried that even with stellar LSAT scores, she might not get into the law school of her choice. The openness of MOOCs allowed her to study a subject she was passionate about without these risks, costs, and commitments. But what, exactly, does "open" mean in this context, and how did it allow Mary to pursue her interest in the law?

MOOC providers most commonly use the term "open" in the acronym to mean that MOOCs are free of the cost and entrance requirements typical of university courses. Yet this understanding falls somewhat short of the ideals of the open education movement, which is based on the belief that open access, open educational resources, and open scholarship will allow "individuals who might otherwise never have the opportunity to experience post-secondary learning a free and open chance to participate" (Wiley and Green 2012, 88). The open education movement has a "strong ideological basis rooted in an ethical pursuit for democratization, fundamental human rights, equality, and justice" (Veletsianos and Kimmons 2012, 172) and views openness as a means of achieving democratic and socially valuable ends. In 2001, MIT took a step toward fulfilling such aims with their OpenCourseWare initiative, which made instructional materials from a number of courses freely available online. Khan Academy, which Siemens (2013) describes as a "quasi-MOOC," took this yet a step further by adding a course-like structure to its collection of open access videos, activities, and assessments. MOOCs, having evolved from these two initiatives, brought together freely available materials from universities and bundled them into a format resembling traditional university courses.

Declaring 2012 the "Year of the MOOC" (Pappano 2012), the *New York Times* touted MOOCs as a means of providing greater access to learning opportunities (particularly to courses offered by highly ranked universities) and as a step toward broadening participation and access to education. When Coursera began in 2012, its website described its vision as providing the world with "access to the world-class education that has so far been available only to a select few." For lifelong learners like Mary without the time or financial means to take more traditional courses, MOOCs allow access to world-renowned professors. For others, MOOCs may be their only access to higher education. In another headline-grabbing piece, the *New York Times* shared the inspirational story of Battushig Myanganbayar, a 15-year-old from Mongolia whose perfect score in MIT's Circuits and Electronics MOOC earned him the opportunity to attend MIT in person (Pappano 2013). Similar stories continued to garner media interest: in 2015, the *Chronicle of Higher Education* interviewed Jima Ngei, who lived in Nigeria and had completed more than 250 MOOCs (Digital Campus 2015). All these aspirational stories align with the stated goal of the MOOC movement, which according to edX president Anant Agarwal, "is to educate a billion people around the world" (edX 2012) and make education "borderless, gender-blind, race-blind, class-blind, and bank account-blind" (Agarwal 2013).

Yet, while expanding learning opportunities to those without access is a laudable goal, the accomplishments of learners like Battushig and Jima are far from the norm. For the most part, the learners who take MOOCs are already well served by higher education. Studies have repeatedly shown that MOOC participants are, by and large, highly educated, gainfully employed residents of developed countries (see, e.g., Christensen et al. 2013; Ho et al. 2014; Hansen and Reich 2015). Online learning, no matter how open, cannot reach learners without a computer, access to the internet, support structures to aid their learning/studies, and enough leisure time to develop, let alone pursue, learning goals. As online learning expert John Daniel states, "It is a myth to think that providing not-for-credit open online learning from the USA will address the challenges of expanding higher education in the developing world" (2012, 15).

MOOCs may not live up to edX's claim of making education "borderless," but what of its claims of making it gender, race, class, and bank-account blind? When Hansen and Reich (2015) studied data from all the MOOCs run by Harvard and MIT over a two-year period, including demographic data on more than 160,000 participants, they found that the ratio of male to female participants was similar to those in traditional higher education settings. The implication of this finding is that MOOCs have not made education gender-blind but have rather replicated, or reflected, the inequities of higher education systems. Their study also found that MOOCs, rather than being class- or income-blind, tended to enroll students who lived in more affluent neighborhoods and had higher than average levels of education. This was particularly true for learners who completed the course and earned a certificate, something for which MOOCs are increasingly charging a fee.

Although Mary was happy to pay $60 for the "verified certificate" that she proudly hung on her wall, even a nominal cost is prohibitive to many, and fees of any sort negate the premise that the "openness" in MOOCs means being free of charge.

Although Battushig remained a fan of MOOCs after becoming a student at MIT and still took them in his spare time, he also had some criticisms that point to some of their limitations (Young 2016). One of these was that being able to take a MOOC offered by one of the world's leading universities is not the same as taking an actual course there, most importantly in the ability to meet with a professor. In MOOCs, access to a professor is generally limited to watching prerecorded lectures; although some MOOC professors interact with students via forums and a few offer office hours, rarely are they accessible in the same way they would be to a fee-paying student in a physical or online classroom. As we saw in chapter 7, interaction and community are central to effective online learning, and even though some learners feel like they learned a lot, the lack of interaction between learners and instructors may not only leave some learners behind but may also exclude the contributions that faculty members bring to interaction, such as scaffolding and correcting misconceptions. Another of Battushig's observations revealed what may be a certain naïveté in the ideals and claims of both the MOOC and the open movement: "I think at the peak of the MOOC, everyone was excited about the opportunity to learn more. That's an amazing thing. It's the same as, you're provided the free book, and you can just read it a lot of times. But in those books, no one teaches you how to solve problems in your community, and that itself will discourage underprivileged people from taking a MOOC. For the underprivileged people, the learning more is almost like a punishment because it reminds you more about the resource restrictions."

...

- MOOCs are partially aligned with the open education movement.
- While some learners may be successful with MOOCs, for the most part these initiatives have not "democratized" education on a global scale as originally predicted and anticipated by proponents.
- Some research shows that MOOCs reflect and replicate existing inequities, lending support to the argument that technocentric solutions are rarely sufficient to address structural issues.

References

Agarwal, A. 2013. "Online Universities: It's Time for Teachers to Join the Revolution." *The Guardian: The Observer*, June 15. http://www.theguardian.com/education/2013/jun/15/university-education-online-mooc.

Christensen, G., Steinmetz, A., Alcorn, B., Bennett, A., Woods, D., and Emanuel, E. J. 2013. "The MOOC Phenomenon: Who Takes Massive Open Online Courses and Why?" *SSRN*, November 6. http://papers.ssrn.com/sol3/papers.cfm?abstract_id=2350964.

Daniel, J. 2012. "Making Sense of MOOCs: Musings in a Maze of Myth, Paradox and Possibility." *Journal of Interactive Media in Education* 3: 1–28.

Digital Campus. 2015. "250 MOOCs and Counting: One Man's Educational Journey." *The Chronicle of Higher Education: The Digital Campus*, April 20. http://chronicle.com/article/250-MOOCsCounting-One/229397.

edX. 2012. "EdX: Future of Online Education Is Now." YouTube video, 3:01. Posted August 9, 2012. https://www.youtube.com/watch?v=MJZN7o0YS0o.

Hansen, J. D., and Reich, J. 2015. "Democratizing Education? Examining Access and Usage Patterns in Massive Open Online Courses." *Science* 350 (6265): 1245–1248.

Ho, A. D., Reich, J., Nesterko, S. O., Seaton, D. T., Mullaney, T., Waldo, J., and Chuang, I. 2014. "HarvardX and MITx: The First Year of Open Online Courses." HarvardX and MITx Working Paper No. 1. Harvard University, Cambridge, MA. http://harvardx.harvard.edu/multiple-course-report.

Pappano, L. 2012. "Year of the MOOC." *New York Times*, November 2. http://www.nytimes.com/2012/11/04/education/edlife/massive-open-online-courses-are-multiplying-at-a-rapid-pace.html?pagewanted=all&_r=0.

Pappano, L. 2013. "The Boy Genius of Ulan Bator." *New York Times*, September 13. http://www.nytimes.com/2013/09/15/magazine/the-boy-genius-of-ulan-bator.html.

Siemens, G. 2013. "Massive Open Online Courses: Innovation in Education?" In *Open Educational Resources: Innovation, Research and Practice*, edited by R. McGreal, W. Kinuthia, and S. Marshall, 5–15. Vancouver: Commonwealth of Learning.

Veletsianos, G., and Kimmons, R. 2012. "Assumptions and Challenges of Open Scholarship." *International Review of Research in Open and Distributed Learning* 13 (4): 166–189.

Wiley, D., and Green, C. 2012. "Why Openness in Education?" In *Game Changers: Education and Information Technologies*, edited by D. Oblinger, 81–89. Washington, DC: Educause.

Young, J. R. 2016. "This Mongolian Teenager Aced a MOOC: Now He Wants to Widen Their Impact." *Chronicle of Higher Education*, May 4. http://chronicle.com/article/This-Mongolian-Teenager-Aced-a/236362?cid=cp34.

16.

The Learner Who Took Advantage of Flexible Learning

The precariously piled stacks of papers covering Erin's desk and the rickety bookshelves groaning with the weight of their contents gave her office a haphazard but cozy feel. "I need cozy on a day like today," she said, turning her webcam to reveal the snow falling outside her window on this cold Canadian winter day.

The 40-year-old academic librarian is a self-confessed "MOOC-aholic" who had first encountered MOOCs a few years prior to our conversation. "There's all this talk of data science in libraries these days—I could pretend to know what it was about for only so long," she joked. "I realized I needed to get up to speed." She decided to take a course and started her search by looking through the courses her employer offered. "They'd be free," she had reasoned, "but it would mean taking a couple hours out of my day each week or spending a whole weekend stuck in a classroom."

A Google search for data science courses took her to the Coursera website, where she found and enrolled in what looked like the perfect course. The course included "videos that explained things really clearly. I sort of skipped through a lot of it. I watched what was useful but not the rest. So, I didn't do the assignments or most of the quizzes, just the questions that were from the parts I watched to see if I had understood it right." Being able to pick and choose the parts of the course that were most relevant to her own needs was important to Erin. With a busy library to run and a teenager and preschooler keeping her hands full at home, Erin's time was precious. "Professional development is hugely important to me," she said, gesturing to the tangled lanyards and name badges from numerous conferences hanging from a hook on her wall. "But it needs to fit into my schedule."

In the hour we spent talking, Erin described the many ways she interacted with these courses to meet her needs. Sometimes, she focused on watching the videos. Other times, she reported, she would drop in or drop out of courses, engaging only with the pieces of content she found most interesting. As the interview drew to a close, Erin listed all the MOOCs she had taken, holding up fingers as she counted. When she had gone through all her fingers and then some, she leaned back in her chair and, laughing, admitted that "all that learning, and I never even completed one entire MOOC. I don't have even one certificate to show for it." Yet what she did have to show for it was, in her mind, more valuable than a piece of paper.

The flexibility to be able to drop in and out, to pick and choose resources, and to complete some but not all learning activities may be particularly appealing to learners taking courses primarily for personal fulfillment or professional development rather than a credential. Yet learner testimonials posted on the "Contact North | Contact Nord" website, Ontario's distance education and training network, reveal that flexibility is also hugely important to learners who are pursuing online credentials and provide snapshots of the variety of ways in which online learning enables such learners to participate in educational endeavors from "anyplace" at "anytime." Kim and Jennifer, for example, reported appreciating that taking online courses allowed them to remain in their home communities rather than uproot their families to pursue their education. Raven valued being able to Skype with peers on her own time, and Dickie praised being able to earn his accounting diploma at his own pace, listening to recordings when he was unable to attend a class session.

...

Like many of the learners cited in the literature on online learning, Erin had a demanding job and busy home life that left her little spare time. During our interview, she was interrupted by a phone call, a colleague at the door, and several texts from her husband who was trying to manage two kids at home on a snow day. It's no wonder she felt that the time commitment of a traditional course was more than she could manage. Online courses offered Erin a structure and sequence but also gave her the flexibility she needed to fit studying and learning into her busy schedule.

The need to provide greater flexibility in higher education offerings and programs has become central to larger discussions within and beyond academia. The stereotype of university students as young, single, well-funded, and free of competing demands on their time is less accurate today than ever before (Selingo 2013; also see chapter 2). Increasing numbers of students enrolled in traditional higher education programs as well as lifelong learners find themselves juggling such responsibilities as young children, aging parents, demanding careers, heavy course loads, or long commutes.

Traditionally, universities or colleges have required students to adapt their lives to accommodate their learning. Academic terms have fixed start and end dates, courses last full semesters, and the curriculum to be covered is determined before students even set foot on campus. Further, classes are usually offered in just one modality, face-to-face or online, requiring students to either travel to campus or take the course online rather than being able to choose how to participate based on their particular needs at different points in time. Such rigidity means that students often must make difficult choices between their education, their careers, their social lives, and their families.

Flexible learning, in contrast, provides students with choices around when, where, and how they learn. Online learning is often heralded as the poster child of flexible learning, as it offers participants flexibility in several key dimensions of the learning experience.

A first kind of flexibility is in when and how students can access a course. Many online courses are designed to be asynchronous, meaning that they can be accessed at virtually any time, allowing learners to participate at times convenient to them. This ability to access a course at any time is further enhanced by the capability to access and participate in it through mobile devices like tablets, laptops, or smartphones. Some students that I interviewed as part of my research described using their tablet to continue their coursework while on vacation or their smartphone to watch course videos while cooking or breastfeeding.

A second dimension of online learning's flexibility is in its content and resources. While the majority of online and face-to-face courses are prescriptive, many in academia have been experimenting with course designs that provide flexibility in how learners participate in a course. For instance, rather than going through a predetermined path through a course, designs might allow for students to self-select from a range of activities that satisfy course requirements and learning outcomes. Students may be able to select writing an op-ed versus creating a video or critiquing a podcast about a topic instead of critiquing a scholarly paper about the same topic.

Including flexibility in course design may mean providing options that make it possible for students to complete courses in varied ways. As Erin reported, she "just skipped through" much of her data science MOOC, watching only those videos that addressed the gaps in her content knowledge and using the assessments as a way to monitor her understanding rather than to achieve a grade. Erin made her choices about what to engage with based on her own preferences and learning needs. But the choices of other individuals my colleagues and I interviewed were more constrained by circumstances. Ryed, who lived in Delhi where broadband and power failed regularly enough to make watching videos nearly impossible, completed the MOOCs he took entirely through engaging with others in the discussion forums. Jenna, whose vision problems made it difficult for her to read text on the screen, chose resources she could print out to read and listen to rather than watch the videos. Though Erin, Ryed, and Jenna were reporting on MOOCs, which increase students' choices about how much of the course to complete and how, flexibility is a design feature that can be built into a variety of course designs, including for-credit online courses *and* for-credit in-person courses.

For all the benefits of flexibility though, the common claim that online learning can happen "anywhere at any time," leading some to advise students that they can do online learning "in their jammies" (Lowenthal and Dunlap 2011), obscures many challenges. While flexible learning is intended to avoid some of the limitations imposed by face-to-face instruction, Kahu, Stephens, Zepke, and Leach (2014, 525) argue that "distance study has not overcome the barriers of space and time" as these students still need to fit their studies into their schedule, face competing demands for their time, and face ongoing challenges in attempting to manage a program of study that purports to be flexible yet still requires requisite attention, scheduling, and monitoring (Kirkwood 2000; Selwyn 2011; Sheail 2018).

Although flexibility may improve access to education, it does not eliminate all barriers. Instead, it brings different kinds of difficulties, most often stemming from students' need to find time and space to study in an already full schedule. As Kirkwood (2000) notes, flexibility is not merely a characteristic of a given learning opportunity but something that students must actively exercise to make the most of the time and space available to them. To this extent, some critics warn that "discourses of 'flexibility' can be understood as forming part of a wider neo-liberal project, one that positions learners as always being in need of new training, new credentialing, in order to fill 'gaps' identified in their 'portfolio of learning' and make them more employable" (Oliver 2015, 371).

...

- Online courses are often flexible in that they accommodate learners needs and schedules, allowing them to juggle multiple responsibilities.
- Even though flexibility is often seen in terms of time and place, other aspects of education can be made more flexible (e.g., choice in assessment, flexible admissions policies that value prior experiences).

- Flexibility isn't unproblematic: it imagines learners who are autonomous and places the responsibility on them to be flexible. Institutions should pursue policies and approaches to support the flexibility that they are inviting learners to embrace.

References

Kahu, E., Stephens, C., Zepke, N., and Leach, L. 2014. "Space and Time to Engage: Mature-Aged Distance Students Learn to Fit Study into Their Lives." *International Journal of Lifelong Education* 33 (4): 523–540.

Kirkwood, A. 2000. "Learning at Home with Information and Communication Technologies." *Distance Education* 21 (2): 248–259.

Lowenthal, P. R., and Dunlap, J. C. 2011. "You Can Do It in Your Jammies, and Other Things We Should Never Say about Learning Online." In *The CU Online Handbook*, edited by P. R. Lowenthal, D. Thomas, A. Thai, B. Yuhnke, M. Edwards, and C. Gasell, 9–14. Raleigh, NC: Lulu Enterprises.

Oliver, M. 2015. "From Openness to Permeability: Reframing Open Education in Terms of Positive Liberty in the Enactment of Academic Practices." *Learning, Media and Technology* 40 (3): 365–384.

Selingo, J. 2013. *College (Un)bound: The Future of Higher Education and What It Means for Students*. New York: Houghton Mifflin.

Selwyn, N. 2011. "'Finding an Appropriate Fit for Me': Examining the (In)flexibilities of International Distance Learning." *International Journal of Lifelong Education* 30 (3): 367–383.

Sheail, P. 2018. "The Digital University and the Shifting Time-Space of the Campus." *Learning, Media and Technology* 43 (1): 56–69.

17.

The Learner of the Future

It's the year 2035. Recently, Amina became interested in art history. She is intrigued about the ways that people create art, ranging from paint to digital art. Since her visit to the National Gallery of Canada on her vacation to Ottawa last year, she's been asking Jiri, her digital companion and assistant, many questions about these technologies. What "makes" art? Why have people stopped creating certain types of art? How do artists make a living? Jiri easily and tirelessly provided the information that was asked of him, of course, but Amina was looking for more than information. As Jiri projected artifacts from the past, videos of art being created, and sounds from a long time ago, Amina yearned for more. While that information may have been sufficient for some, she wanted to understand the intricacies of art, its relationship to sociocultural developments, and its impact on people and systems globally. She felt that a more nuanced understanding would help her make sense of her relationship to the world she was inhabiting as well as enable her to improve her life in many other ways:

morally, socially, and financially. "After all," she reasoned, "art and people impact one another, and if I can understand our relationship with art, I may understand the world better."

In 2035—similar to 2020—people have a wide array of options for online learning. Amina decides to pursue an online education by choice, rather than out of need or lack of options. She already has a close relationship with a local university that will help her develop a program of study that fits her needs. She meets with a program advisor to help her develop a personalized program of study that is based on her current knowledge, skills, and competencies; her aspirations; and the advisor's expert knowledge of the field, learning outcomes associated with studying art history, and data from many other learners worldwide who have participated in similar programs. When it's time to start the program a few weeks after that initial meeting, the final schedule and associated learning outcomes have been informed by both people and machines working together to develop a plan that is not only personalized but informed by the latest science of learning.

Amina's plan—which may or may not be similar to those of others—looks like this: Based on her current skills and knowledge, she is placed in a course with 12 other students. Some of them are what one would consider nontraditional students, in their thirties and forties with years of work experience and many with family responsibilities. The course is shared with numerous other universities and organizations and is developed on an ad hoc basis around outcomes and needs. While Amina's peers vary in age, geographical location, and home organization (e.g., some are at a different university, one works for the municipal government, and one is an emerging artist at a K-12 school), they are supported by two instructors and two student success professionals, who are in turn supported by learning designers and a wide range of technologies, including a Jiri-like assistant that aggregates and synthesizes content on a continuous basis and advises on assessment practices. This blend of human and nonhuman instructional staff is typical at this institution. Amina's first course "meets" synchronously and asynchronously using technologies that instill a sense of presence and aim to help people feel supported and valued, even if they live in different countries, even if they speak different languages, even if they use different devices. "Distance education" and "online learning" are terms of a different era. The demarcation between real and virtual is long gone, and by now, technology is designed with a people-first approach, recognizing ethical concerns that researchers raised decades ago.

In the course itself, Amina investigates art from the 1800s, participates in simulations of its creation, and explores the tools used to produce it. She asks questions of peers and technologies alike, sometimes getting together with peers to discuss an assignment over coffee and other times working by herself on a project. The information that students need to know is easy to generate and provide, and, as a result, the course focuses on helping them apply procedural knowledge in a variety of contexts. Each individual's assessments are also developed on a personalized basis, a result of the aforementioned collaboration between people and machines. Though this particular course is nine weeks long, the rest of Amina's courses vary in duration: some are three weeks long and others may be as long as nineteen weeks.

When Amina completes the course, she will once again meet with her program advisor to examine her plan. Courses, learning objectives, and desired skills and knowledge may or may not change, but once she's ready, she'll enroll in a second course and the process will start all over again. As with the first course, Amina's learning experience will be "high touch," encompass the same kind of frequent interactions with her peers and instructors, and invite her to engage actively in her learning.

...

I am generally wary of predictions about the future of education, as I have heard and read too many of them in the mass media, conference keynotes, and trade publications. These predictions almost invariably (1) envision a future that is so far into the future that any failed prediction could be explained away by changes that have occurred in the time that it takes to arrive at that future; (2) highlight the transformational and disruptive role that technology will play in this future; and (3) offer either a dystopian or, more typically, a utopian vision of the future of education. Arguably, the same criticisms could be leveled at my own narrative above, but I offer it as speculative rather than predictive. While I don't believe that this future will necessarily become a reality, I do think that aspects of it are probably close to what a typical future learning experience imbued with technology might look like, providing us with an opportunity to ask the following questions: Is this a future we want? Is this the future we are striving toward? What would a better future look like?

In describing future trends in online learning, a number of commentators and researchers focus on the potential impact of technology. Although the predicted impact of these technologies is often based on beliefs rather than systematic evidence (Selwyn 2013; Kimmons 2014), the integration of emerging technologies in education seems inevitable, if not already occurring. Recent researchers have identified artificial intelligence, virtual and augmented reality, and high-fidelity simulations as the technologies that seem most likely to have a future impact on online learning, which I imagine will soon be joined by a variety of other technologies that have not yet been developed. Such technologies are expected to support and give rise to a variety of new practices that have also gathered attention in the field, such as the use of learning analytics for making data-driven decisions, algorithms that automate a variety of processes (such as assigning students in groups and generating personalized assessments), and options for reducing the cost of education and expanding instructors' abilities to use educational content.

Yet, in imagining the future of education, a number of researchers have also called upon educators to place greater emphasis on demographic, political, economic, social, and cultural factors (e.g., OECD 2018) that are likely to affect not only models of educational provision but also the roles of students, university personnel, and institutions in our society. For instance, Kim (2019) wonders whether we have adequately contemplated "the relationship between climate change, the growth of extreme weather events and the future of learning" and asks "What will the combination of unprecedented wealth accumulation and wealth inequality mean for learning in 2069?" The recommendations of researchers and commentators examining the education of the future are varied. They range from advising practitioners to pay greater attention to the field of learning sciences in order to develop research-informed learning environments (e.g., Sawyer 2014) to recommending to universities to streamline their offerings and restructure their colleges and personnel (e.g., Kamenetz 2013).

One way to explore the complexities associated with the future of online learning is to contemplate what Amina's story leaves out. For instance, it does not address the probable costs of the various human and technological supports that mediate her learning experience and assist her in personalizing and succeeding in her studies. Perhaps Amina does not need to be concerned about the cost of her education, either because she has the financial means necessary to pursue her education or because education in the country in which she lives is now low-cost or free. Perhaps her employer and partner also support her aspirations: her employer by providing paid time off and accommodations as needed, and her partner by taking on greater responsibilities at home to allow her time to pursue her studies. A defining characteristic of this future, therefore, seems to be a constellation of broader support from Amina's family, employer, university, and government. The support provided by these other actors is as significant to her experience and success as her inner desire to pursue higher learning and is as consequential to the future of online learning as the particular technologies or pedagogies that may be employed.

What Amina's story also reveals, therefore, is that this particular future rests upon assumptions about broader forces that impact upon online learning. For instance, if some women's online studies continue to be interrupted by caregiving responsibilities that remain unchanged when women become students, and if some learners can't pursue online education due to financial or linguistic constraints, the future described in the above narrative is likely to be available to only a select group of people. For too long, this reality suggests, the field of online learning has focused upon micro aspects of education, such as the pedagogical decisions surrounding online instruction or the models needed to scale online learning, without adequate attention to broader forces that shape online education's use, success, design, and future.

Although I have offered Amina's story to help us consider what the future may hold, it is not intended to suggest that there is a single kind of online student or a single future for online learning. Instead, there are multiple futures, and some are better than others. These better futures are more equitable than the alternatives—more empowering, compassionate, and sensitive to student needs—and designed to capitalize on the potential of online learning to not be a "less than" form of learning than face-to-face education. Futures that employ sophisticated instructional techniques but are reserved only for a select few who can afford them, or that pursue online learning as a business strategy rather than a learning venture, or that end up benefiting some students at the cost of placing more people in precarious employment, are likely to be worse. None of these futures, however, are inevitable. The question we need to ask ourselves: what futures should we create?

...

- Be suspect of predictions about the future of online learning and the impact of educational technology on education, and question the assumptions behind those predictions.
- Ask: who will benefit from this imagined future?
- Consider the broader forces that shape online education: economics, politics, sociocultural factors, and so on.

References

Kamenetz, A. 2013. "$1 Trillion and Rising: A Plan for a $10K Degree." *Third Way*, September 25. https://www.thirdway.org/report/1-trillion-and-rising-a-plan-for-a-10k-degree.

Kim, J. 2019. "Learning in 2069?" *Inside Higher Ed* (blog), January 9. https://www.insidehighered.com/digital-learning/blogs/technology-and-learning/what-will-learning-look-2069-dont-focus-technology.

Kimmons, R. 2014. "Emergent Forms of Technology-Influenced Scholarship." In *Encyclopedia of Information Science and Technology*, edited by M. Khosrow-Pour, 3rd ed. 2481–2488. Hershey, PA: IGI Global.

OECD. 2018. *The Future of Education and Skills: Education 2030*. Paris: OECD. http://www.oecd.org/education/2030/E2030%20 Position%20Paper%20(05.04.2018).pdf.

Sawyer, K., ed. 2014. "Introduction: The New Science of Learning." In *The Cambridge Handbook of the Learning Sciences*, 1–20. 2nd ed. New York: Cambridge University Press.

Selwyn, N. 2013. *Distrusting Educational Technology: Critical Questions for Changing Times*. New York: Routledge.

Conclusion

If you had any doubt before, I hope this book has helped convince you that online learning is an endeavor that "keeps it interesting." To some commentators, educators, and members of the public, the field is synonymous with diversity, inclusion, and compassion. To others, it is an anathema, a vehicle through which market forces will inevitably penetrate education and disempower the university and its mission in society. I hope that the stories and accompanying analyses have increased your appreciation of the ways it can be either and, by highlighting the intricacies and tensions of this exciting field, encouraged you to explore it further. As interest in this area continues to grow, I am confident that developments—both positive and negative—will be worthwhile to follow.

If you're reading this book because you are considering becoming an online student, I hope it has provided some insight into what it may be like to study in this modality. If, however, you are reading this as a higher education professional exploring the merits of online education as a strategic move for your university, contemplating offering an online program in your college, or debating the ills and virtues of online education with colleagues and hoping to glean a convincing argument or two, I implore you to return to the premise of this book and keep the learners in mind. As you investigate and ponder these options, ask yourself questions that consider the learners they may impact, such as the following:

- Who are the learners in the proposed online program?
- What do they need and why?
- Who has decided that an online degree or course is needed, and what are their motivations?
- Have learners been consulted in the development of this program?

One critique I often hear about online education is that its advocates are eager to propose online education as a solution for other people's children but not for their own. Perhaps you can use a version of this critique to improve an online education initiative by putting yourself in the shoes of the learner and asking yourself the following questions,

- If I had a choice, would I enroll in this program? Why? Why not?
- If I did not have a choice and had to enroll in this program, what would make this program better for me? What would make this program better for people who are different than me?
- If I wouldn't enroll in this program, do I expect others to do so? Why?

But even if we believe that we know and understand learners and their aspirations and desires, it may be worthwhile to pause and actually talk to them, invite them to take part in designing, developing, and improving online learning.

In short, we need to remain humble about the boundaries of our understanding of other people's realities. Indeed, we may know how to teach and how to craft curricula, but the individuals we teach are not merely students. They may also be parents, workers, stay-at-home fathers, heads of companies, caregivers, or dealing with a variety of issues that we aren't aware of or have never experienced. By approaching our students, our learning designs, and our educational offerings with a sense of humility, we may be able to enact online education in the spirit of its most worthy aspirational goals.

INDEX

Page numbers in *italics* refer to figures.

communities of practice, 91–92
comparison of online and face-to-face courses, 11–18
Contact North/Contact Nord, 150–51
control-value model of emotion, 81, 82–83
convenience of courses, 36–38
Cormier, D., 73
Corrigan-Gibbs, H., 100–101
cost efficiency of courses, 37
Coursera, 8, 144, 149–50
co-writing technologies, 116
Crawford, K., 90
Croft, N., 69
Croxton, R. A., 42, 45
Cuban, L., 53
cultural diversity, 55
Cutrell, E., 100–101

Dalton, A., 69
Daniel, John, 145
Daston, C., 51
data collection and ownership, 119–20
data trails on digital platforms, 7–8
degree completion, 49–56
Delahunty, J., 35–36, 80, 82
demographic data on performance, 53–54
demographic trends. See nontraditional learners
Dennen, V. P., 92
digital divides, 52–56
digital literacies, 59–65
digital note-taking, 115–20
Dillon, J., 82, 83
discomfort with campus environments, 37–38, 87–88
discussion boards, 87–88
disparities between learners, 51–52
distance from students, 3–4
Downes, S., 134
Dron, J., 34–35, 38, 125

dropout rates, 5, 46–47
dropping out, 41–47, 83

Education Advisory Board, 38
education at scale, 108
emotion, role of, in learning, 77–84
employment, as motivation, 21–22, 35–36
engagement: forms of, 93; with peers, 12, 71–74; social media tools for, 122–27. See also interaction; participation
enrollments: in Canada, 25; digital skills required for, 63; ease of, 50–51; in MOOCs, 1, 23, 38; in North America, 23–24; in US, 24–25, 28–29; worldwide, 22–23, 26–27
environmental factors: in attrition, 43, 44; in self-directed learning, 136–37
extrinsic motivation, 35

face-to-face courses, online courses compared to, 11–18
Ferguson, K., 44–45
flexibility: demand for, 35, 36–38, 51; maximizing, 70; of online learning, 149–55
for-profit colleges, predatory, 13–14
Fox, H. L., 37–38
Frick, T. W., 45
Fusch, G. E., 97
Fusch, P. I., 97
future of education, ideas on, 157–63

Gannon, K., 14
George, A. S., 34–35, 38
Glister, P., 62
Goel, Ashok, 109
Goode, J., 52
Grant, M., 69
Gupta, N., 100–101